Building an ITIL®-based Service Management Department

London: TSO

information & publishing solutions

Published by TSO (The Stationery Office) and available from:

Online
www.tsoshop.co.uk

Mail, Telephone, Fax & E-mail
TSO
PO Box 29, Norwich NR3 1GN
Telephone orders/General enquiries: 0870 6005522
Fax orders: 0870 6005533
E-mail: customer.services@tso.co.uk
Textphone: 0870 240 3701

TSO Shops
16 Arthur Street, Belfast BT1 4GD
028 9023 8451
Fax 028 9023 5401
71 Lothian Road, Edinburgh EH3 9AZ
0870 606 5566
Fax 0870 606 5588

TSO@Blackwell and other Accredited Agents

© The Stationery Office 2008

All rights reserved. No part of this publication may be reproduced, stored in a retrieval system, or transmitted in any form or by any means, electronic, mechanical, photocopying, recording or otherwise without the permission of the publisher.

Applications for reproduction should be made in writing to The Stationery Office Limited, St Crispins, Duke Street, Norwich NR3 1PD.

The information contained in this publication is believed to be correct at the time of manufacture. Whilst care has been taken to ensure that the information is accurate, the publisher can accept no responsibility for any errors or ommissions or for changes to the details given.

Malcolm Fry has asserted his moral rights under the Copyright, Designs and Patents Act 1988, to be identified as the author of this work.

ITIL® is a Registered Trade Mark of the Office of Government Commerce in the United Kingdom and other countries

The Swirl logo™ is a Trade Mark of the Office of Government Commerce

A CIP catalogue record for this book is available from the British Library

A Library of Congress CIP catalogue record has been applied for

First published 2008

ISBN 9780113310968

Printed in the United Kingdom by The Stationery Office, London.

N5796707 c15 06/08

Contents

List of figures and tables v

Acknowledgements vii

1 **A classic departmental structure** 1
   1.1 The eternal ITIL triangle 3
   1.2 Service Management department structure 4

2 **Overview of a step-by-step approach** 13
   2.1 Why a step-by-step approach? 15
   2.2 The steps 15

3 **Step 1 – Preparing the basics** 17
   3.1 A project approach 19
   3.2 Selecting a project team 19
   3.3 Collating current materials 20
   3.4 Other ITIL projects 20

4 **Step 2 – Defining departmental parameters** 21
   4.1 Creating a mission statement 23
   4.2 Introduction to departmental parameters 23
   4.3 Creating the parameters 24

5 **Step 3 – Identifying primary ITIL Fundamental Tasks** 27
   5.1 Definition of the primary ITIL Fundamental Tasks 29
   5.2 Identifying the ITIL Fundamental Tasks 30
   5.3 Documenting the ITIL Fundamental Tasks 31

6 **Step 4 – Identifying non-ITIL Fundamental Tasks** 33
   6.1 Definition of a non-ITIL Fundamental Task 35
   6.2 Examples of non-ITIL Fundamental Tasks 35
   6.3 Preparing to locate non-ITIL Fundamental Tasks 37
   6.4 Identifying the non-ITIL Fundamental Tasks 37
   6.5 Documenting non-ITIL tasks 38

7 **Step 5 – Rationalizing the Fundamental Tasks** 43
   7.1 Rating the tasks 45
   7.2 Reviewing and grading tasks 45
   7.3 Removing the Rejected Fundamental Tasks 47
   7.4 Meeting the departmental parameters 48
   7.5 Documenting the rationalized Fundamental Tasks 50

8	**Step 6 – Creating Associated Fundamental Task Packs**	**51**
	8.1 Definition of an Associated Fundamental Task Pack	53
	8.2 Benefits of Associated Fundamental Task Packs	54
	8.3 Establishing Associated Fundamental Task Packs	54
	8.4 Deciding on your final Associated Fundamental Task Packs	59
	8.5 Meeting the departmental parameters	59
	8.6 Documenting the Associated Fundamental Task Packs	61
9	**Step 7 – Constructing your Service Management department**	**63**
	9.1 Influencing factors	65
	9.2 Arranging your AFTPs into Departmental Units	65
	9.3 Naming Departmental Units	67
	9.4 Finalizing the construction	69
	9.5 Departmental characteristics	70
10	**Step 8 – Organizational plans and charts**	**75**
	10.1 Organizational plans	78
	10.2 Organizational charts	81
	10.3 Summary	82
11	**Step 9 – Resourcing your Service Management department**	**83**
	11.1 Job descriptions	85
	11.2 Processes and work instructions	86
	11.3 Service Management technology	87
	11.4 Summary	89
12	**Implementing your Service Management department**	**91**
	12.1 Preparing a phased plan	93
Appendix A: Example of an ITIL version 2 departmental template		**97**
Appendix B: Example of an ITIL version 3 departmental template		**101**
Index		**105**

List of figures and tables

Figures

Figure 1.1	Blend of people, processes and technology
Figure 1.2	Ancient Egyptian social structure
Figure 1.3	Comparing ancient to modern
Figure 1.4	Modern organization versus IT Service Management department
Figure 1.5	Service Management department structure
Figure 1.6	Multi-level Service Desk
Figure 2.1	The steps to success
Figure 3.1	Repetitive step group
Figure 4.1	Example of an Associated Fundamental Task Pack
Figure 4.2	Logical grouping of Fundamental Tasks
Figure 4.3	Example of a mission statement chart
Figure 5.1	ITIL v3 Fundamental Tasks
Figure 5.2	Example of Fundamental Task documentation
Figure 6.1	Non-ITIL Fundamental Tasks
Figure 6.2	ITIL v3 and non-ITIL Fundamental Tasks
Figure 7.1	Rationalizing the Fundamental Tasks
Figure 7.2	Current and Planned Fundamental Tasks
Figure 7.3	Current and Planned Fundamental Tasks grouped by ratings
Figure 7.4	Fundamental Tasks and departmental parameters comparison spreadsheet
Figure 8.1	Example of an Associated Fundamental Task Pack
Figure 8.2	Multiple examples of Associated Fundamental Task Packs
Figure 8.3	Integrity of Service Management
Figure 8.4	Legal and contractual
Figure 8.5	Financial
Figure 8.6	Customer communications
Figure 8.7	Customer information
Figure 8.8	Introduction of new services
Figure 8.9	Technology and operational activities
Figure 8.10	Demand, capacity and availability
Figure 8.11	Managing events, incidents and problems
Figure 8.12	Managing change
Figure 8.13	Service improvement
Figure 8.14	Other Fundamental Tasks
Figure 8.15	AFTPs and departmental parameters comparison spreadsheet
Figure 9.1	Grouping AFTPs into Departmental Units
Figure 9.2	A complete Departmental Unit
Figure 9.3	Naming the Departmental Units
Figure 9.4	Final department structure
Figure 9.5	Alternative departmental template
Figure 9.6	Departmental characteristics: the eight key questions
Figure 9.7	Departmental characteristics
Figure 10.1	Alternative departmental template plan with added AFTPs
Figure 10.2	Organization plan at management level
Figure 10.3	Organizational plan for Service Integrity
Figure 10.4	Organizational plan for Service Planning
Figure 10.5	Organizational plan for Service Operations

Figure 10.6 Organizational plan for Service Support

Figure 10.7 Migrating from an organizational plan to an organizational chart

Figure 11.1 Process metrics

Figure 12.1 Phased approach map

Figure 12.2 ITIL v2 to v3 transitioning phased approach map

Figure A.1 Example of an ITIL version 2 departmental template

Figure B.1 Example of an ITIL version 3 departmental template

Figure B.2 Dissipated Service Management disciplines

Tables

Table 6.1 ITIL v3 and non-ITIL Fundamental Tasks

Table 9.1 Departmental structural levels and their importance

Table 12.1 Implementation plan

Acknowledgements

Author

Malcolm Fry

Reviewers

Steve Ackland	Aim4Gain, UK
Matthew Burrows	BSMimpact, UK
David Jones	Plan-Net, UK
Thomas Law	HP, UK
John Sowerby	DHL, UK
Dean Taylor	VEGA, UK
Paul Wigzel	UK

A classic departmental structure

1 A classic departmental structure

1.1 THE ETERNAL ITIL TRIANGLE

Since its first appearance, the Information Technology Infrastructure Library (ITIL) has championed successful Service Management (SM) as the result of a finely balanced cocktail of people, processes and technology.

Figure 1.1 Blend of people, processes and technology

Just like the creation of a new cocktail, for most organizations success comes from experimentation, patience and vision. However, the results of a failed cocktail can be thrown into the sink, but we cannot dispose of failed Service Management experiments – we have to live with them. Therefore we need to have full cognisance of all three components – people, processes and technology. There are many sources to help select and implement the best technology, as there are for designing and implementing processes, which explains why so many organizations have had success in these areas. It is the people component that is often lacking in substance.

There are many education and training specialists who supply excellent courses about ITIL and Information Technology Service Management (ITSM). There is also a well-constructed ITIL certification scheme so that ITSM professionals can gain recognized industry status within their area of expertise. Education, training and certification produce skilled and motivated people, but where will they fit into the IT department? Should there be a separate Service Management department? If so, who should be in that department? Should Problem, Incident and Change Management all be performed by the same team?

These are interesting questions, but like the processes and technology components, a Service Management department (SMD) requires planning and careful specification. It is not possible to produce one all-embracing Service Management department template, although several straw models can be used as a guide. The final design of your SMD will depend on which ITIL components you have implemented, the degree to which you have implemented them, and the level of maturity that you have planned to achieve from your ITIL implementation.

In short, education and training are not enough; the objective must be to build an SMD that will harness and maximize the knowledge and skills of your Service Management staff, while at the same time deliver cost-effective and robust services to the SMD clients, customers and users.

1.2 SERVICE MANAGEMENT DEPARTMENT STRUCTURE

Building a successful department requires far more than an organization chart, which is useful to show structure and reporting levels, but does not show how the department achieves its goals or responsibilities. Before creating an organization chart, it is important to plan the sub-structure of your department.

1.2.1 An ancient approach

When planning for this publication I searched far and wide for departmental models and templates that I could use to illustrate how a successful department could be constructed. Although I found many examples, most of them focused on a particular type of department, or were examples of existing departments, or were simply organization charts. I then realized that these were all useful but lacked a sub-structure, i.e. something that shows the nature and character of a department. It was at this point that I remembered a book I read some time ago that described the social structure of ancient Egypt. This may not sound relevant here, but it described how the sub-structure of Egypt was constructed, and illustrated why Egypt was so well organized for over 4,000 years. If we look at this structure we can see how it is still relevant today.

Before we analyse Figure 1.2, it is important to remember that it is the roles that matter, not the position in the hierarchy. As you can see, the social structure represents a pyramid, which is very appropriate for ancient Egypt. We will look at each level and then compare each of these levels to a modern departmental sub-structure.

Figure 1.2 Ancient Egyptian social structure

- **Pharaoh** He was the figurehead, in fact a god, for the ancient Egyptians, and the whole structure was built to support and protect the Pharaoh. In return for supporting the Pharaoh they entrusted him with many responsibilities, such as protection from a foreign threat or feeding them during a famine.
- **Government officials (nobles and priests)** These officials supported the Pharaoh and were responsible for seeing that all the tasks required to run the country were successfully completed, including collecting taxes and other revenues. They would take instructions from the Pharaoh and report to the Pharaoh accordingly.
- **Soldiers** Soldiers fought in wars or quelled domestic uprisings and protected the Pharaoh. Soldiers also served as supervisors during long periods of peace, controlling the peasants, farmers and slaves who were involved in building such structures as pyramids and public buildings.

Already we can see a pattern emerging: there is a boss (the Pharaoh), senior managers, government officials and local managers.

- **Scribes** These people would document all the decisions and actions decreed by the Pharaoh and were managed by the government officials. Documentation, like modern Service Management knowledge, was very important to the ancient Egyptian structure. The scribes kept meticulous records on a wide range of subjects, including the success of the pharaohs, taxes, finances, stock levels, court judgments and regulations.
- **Merchants** Along with the storekeepers, the merchants would buy the goods produced by the artisans or bartered by traders. This is an important level because without trade any nation would struggle. The merchants were often seen as the face of the structure because they travelled and communicated with their customers and suppliers to resell the goods purchased from the artisans.
- **Artisans** These were skilled workers producing items such as fine clothes, jewellery, weapons and pottery. Every country, or department, requires skilled professionals to produce their most valued products.

Again we can see a picture emerging, because the volumes and types of products would depend on the sales by the merchants and storekeepers, which would be documented by the scribes (for taxes), supervised by the soldiers, made to specifications demanded by the government officials to meet a request from the Pharaoh.

- **Farmers** Farmers did the typical farming duties, such as tending the fields and raising animals, but apart from these farming duties they also kept canals and reservoirs in good order for irrigation. They were also required to work in the stone quarries and helped to build the royal monuments – certainly a busy life. The farmers were a critical level in the structure, because without food there would be no Pharaoh.
- **Support** At the base of the social structure were people who performed the supporting activities. In Egyptian times they were often called the slaves and servants. They were used for all types of menial manual labour, but were important to the success of Egypt because without these tasks the social structure would collapse.

So there is the social structure of ancient Egypt. Each of the layers is just as important as the layers above and below it. It is the relationships between the layers that are important, because if you remove any one layer, or tamper with the relationships, the whole structure collapses. Also notice the pyramid shape in Figure 1.2: this is significant because, as a general rule, if you start from the top and work down, fewer people are required to perform the tasks at the higher levels than at the lower levels of the structure.

Another key factor was social mobility – people could ascend the economic and social ladder. It was possible for a boy born to parents low down in the structure to work his way up into the higher ranks of the government. Boys who learned to read and write could become scribes, then go on to gain employment in the government. Families would save their money to send their sons to village schools to learn trades. Similarly in modern business today, you can start off at the bottom of an organization and rise to the top. Many parents help their children to jump above the lower levels of the structure by sending them to college or university to obtain qualifications. Even so, some of the most successful business people have started at the lowest level.

We will soon see how the social structure of ancient Egypt applies to modern businesses and especially to Service Management. The keys to success for the Egyptians were their faith in the Pharaoh and the fact that everyone knew exactly what they had to do to contribute to success.

1.1.1 Applying the ancient to the modern

It is easy to see how the social structure worked so well for the ancient Egyptians, but can we relate it to modern departmental structure? The answer is 'yes', it can be applied extremely well. Let us start by looking at Figure 1.3.

Figure 1.3 Comparing ancient to modern

A quick glance at the Figure 1.3 shows how well the ancient structure reflects the structure of a modern organization. As we will see later, this approach can be very successfully scaled to meet the demands of a Service Management department. For now let us compare the two approaches.

Pharaoh/the organization

The Pharaoh was the figurehead for Egypt; similarly, the company or organization is the business figurehead. The organization may not quite be a God, but it is still the reason for the other layers to exist, just like the Pharaoh. However, in return for supporting our organization we expect to have, among other things, job satisfaction, good salaries, career paths and a safe working environment. If we all concentrate on keeping the organization functioning successfully, then we can look forward to a rewarding future. In some companies the CEO/founder can be so powerful that they almost seem like a Pharaoh, e.g. Bill Gates, Michael Dell and Sir Richard Branson.

Government officials/senior management

There is a clear parallel here because senior management, just like the government officials, are charged with not only seeing that all of the tasks required to run the organization are successfully completed, but also with managing finance and other revenues. One key difference is that senior management set the organizational objectives and mission statement and are also responsible for growth, planning and product development. Although some Pharaohs were content to sit back and hand the reins over to their senior government officials, this is not the case with senior managers, who can delegate, but need to ensure that good feedback lines and clear metrics are in place to keep them informed of the daily IT Service Management status.

Soldiers/management

It sounds rather heavy to describe management as soldiers, but in fact their roles are very similar. Building a pyramid required strong management, provided by the soldiers, to ensure that all tasks were completed on time and to the correct specification. There would, of course, be local supervisors to directly oversee the workers, but the soldiers were the key because they provided the strength and discipline. Even though running a Service Management department often seems like building a pyramid every day, it is not – it is more of a never-ending journey. However, just like building a pyramid, ITSM requires strong management to ensure that all daily operational tasks are completed within the stated time frames and that they conform to agreed service levels.

Scribes/auditors and bookkeepers

Scribes were often viewed with suspicion and caution because of the knowledge that they accumulated and the power that they wielded behind the scenes. Few knew more about the true state of Egypt than the scribes. A lazy or crooked scribe could create many problems – for example, if the grain in storage was recorded as higher than the real amount, this error could cause many deaths in a drought if the Nile failed to flood; or a crooked scribe could record the grain as lower than existed and sell the excess. The ancient Egyptians also saw the role of scribe as a knowledge resource that could aid management decision-making – poor information equals poor decisions. These roles are often described as 'back office' functions in modern businesses, but are nonetheless vital. Activities such as security, financial management, Change Management, asset management, governance compliance, third-party management, Knowledge Management and contract management are just as important for an ITSM department as they were for ancient Egypt.

Merchants/sales and marketing

As in any society, the ancient Egyptians produced goods for barter or for sale both domestically and internationally. It was the role of the merchants to find the buyers for the products produced by the artisans and workers and then to sell the goods to those buyers at the best, i.e. lowest, price for either money or in exchange for other goods. This practice has changed little over the last 2,000 years, except that most transactions today are cash-based, although many cultures do still barter. Almost every organization today has its customers who are the target for its sales and marketing; even political parties have their manifestos to sell the services that they will provide if elected. Apart from bartering and selling, merchants also played a valuable role in linking the ancient production process – for example, in the production of clothes, sheep needed to be sheared, wool needed to be prepared, the wool needed to be dyed, then woven, then clothes would be tailored from the resulting cloth, with the merchants being the link between each step by buying and selling at each stage.

ITSM is no different, as IT departments with charge-back can testify. Even those without charge-back know that the money for IT comes from the corporate budget. ITSM is in constant contact with its customers and has a very clear sales role, but equally important is the role that ITSM takes in linking and blending the numerous IT processes on behalf of its customers.

On the face of it, it would seem that ITSM does very little sales and marketing, but the truth is very different. For example, ITSM sells Service Level Agreements (SLAs); Service Desks are the public face of IT; business resource managers speak regularly with their respective business managers; and doesn't every ITSM department use the terms 'customers' or 'clients'? ITSM departments must incorporate sales and marketing if they are to expand the range of services they provide to their customers.

Artisans/skilled (qualified) workers

Apprentices and master craftsmen were well established in ancient Egypt. It took many years of dedication to produce the skills to make something as exquisite as Tutankhamun's death mask. Two points need to be considered here – the passing on of accumulated knowledge, and the testing of pupils to prove that they have attained the necessary skills and knowledge. Over the last few years, the drive towards well-qualified staff has accelerated as we also try to establish a hierarchy of qualified and skilled staff. Staff now accumulate knowledge from their peers, while specialist tutors from universities, colleges and private education companies provide the expert tuition for staff to obtain the certifications to prove that they have acquired the necessary skills and knowledge. Incidentally, if an artisan's work was not up to standard, they could lose their status and/or commissions – was this the same as 'getting the sack'?

Farmers/production and office workers

No country can survive without food, which is why all cultures and countries see farming and food-gathering as a vital task. The more sophisticated the culture, the less time and people are required to gather or produce food; in some cultures it can occupy almost all waking time. The ancient Egyptians were very sophisticated, employing irrigation and fertilization, thus freeing much of the population to concentrate on the other tasks that created the great power of ancient Egypt. Business and organizations are very similar, using technology to improve product build times and quality levels. It is interesting that farmers never get medals, yet without the food that they produce, soldiers would not be able to fight; likewise production staff rarely get the praise they deserve for producing high-quality goods – instead the recognition usually goes to designers or managers. Production and office workers are a vital part of any organization; for example, if parts are not ordered correctly, then products cannot be produced.

Support/back office support

It is easy to look down at this level because it is at the bottom of the social structure, but this can be misguided. For some campaigns in ancient Egypt, the servant/slave water carriers went ahead of the armies so that the troops had fresh water when they arrived at their destination – vital to survival in the desert. Many years ago a CEO of Sony in the UK told me that one of the most important roles in his company was that of the cleaners, because in his opinion a dirty environment creates sloppy working practices; he is probably the only CEO to know all his cleaners by their given names. Back office functions – such as cleaning, decorating, furnishing, reception, receiving and security – may not actually produce products, but are vital in the environment required to produce them.

ITSM, where until recently no qualifications existed, perform back office functions within IT, such as maintaining the Service Desk, operating computers, managing output production and controlling media. Things are starting to change as certification is now available in a range of ITSM-related subjects with ITIL leading the way, aided by industry associations, other best practices, and even universities, which are now offering Masters degrees in Service Management.

1.2.3 Applying the ancient and modern to IT Service Management

So far we have looked at how the ancient Egyptian social structure relates to modern organizations. Now we need to take this a step further and show how it relates to an IT Service Management department.

Figure 1.4 Modern organization versus IT Service Management department

In Figure 1.4, the right-hand column is the same as Figure 1.3, but in the left-hand column the ancient Egyptian structure has been replaced with key layers that relate to an IT Service Management department.

The focal point, the pinnacle, the mission

Without a focal point, Service Management can function but lacks direction and ambition. Every team needs an objective; even a dream team needs a team dream. If the Service Management dream does not exist, or keeps being changed, then Service Management cannot deliver the potential of ITIL v3. Having a vision or mission statement should be the starting point for any project to build a Service Management department, or improve an existing one. This will be discussed in a later chapter.

The key decision level

This is an obvious requirement for any department, but can sometimes be forgotten when building a new department. The answer is to ensure that the key decision level is visible and understood by the whole team. Service Management has two distinct types of decision-making:

- Dynamic risk analysis, requiring fast and accurate decision-making, for processes such as Incident, Problem and Change Management
- Decisions concerning the direction and development of the department, such as recruitment and forward planning.

It is important to clarify both levels of decision-making so that staff and customers are not confused. In the case of departmental decisions, there could be a board of key individuals making the decisions, or the departmental head. Either way, the decisions must be conveyed in an accurate and timely manner. For those dynamic decisions there needs to be clear documentation and formal delegation of authority to those making these decisions.

Putting decisions into practice

By its very nature a Service Management department will action many decisions in a day. Most of these require fast risk analysis and application, but there are also departmental decisions to take into account. The success for Service Management lies in staff knowing how they should implement those decisions. For example, the decision may be to escalate a problem, but how do you put this into practice? The answer is that there should be clear work instructions, along with the necessary training and education, so that staff can put these dynamic decisions into practice with confidence and accuracy. This is essential for Service Management departments, because wrongly actioned decisions can have very serious implications. For putting into practice departmental decisions, it is important for Service Management to employ project management whenever applicable, because not only is it the most efficient method, but it also raises the profile of Service Management within the rest of IT, especially with development.

Documentation and finance

Documentation covers a wide scope in ITIL v3, from Knowledge Management to work instructions and process documentation. Obviously these cannot all be produced or managed at one point, but the strength of Service Management lies in the successful application of its accumulated and documented knowledge. When constructing a Service Management department, it is essential to identify the different sources of knowledge and allocate the appropriate resources to manage that knowledge.

One of the other key roles at the documentation and finance level relates to auditing, conformance, best practices and governance. Service Management has to make sure that all of its roles and processes conform to industry and legal criteria. Some of the processes managed by Service Management perform a guardian role on behalf of IT providers and customers. For example, a service that adheres to Sarbanes-Oxley is progressing through Change Management, but what if the change alters the service so that it no longer adheres to Sarbanes-Oxley? It is the responsibility of the change manager to ensure that changed services remain conformant, and if Service Management owns Change Management then it assumes this responsibility.

Finance appears in many guises, but for Service Management the three largest components are:

- Return on investment (ROI)
- Total cost of ownership (TCO)
- Departmental account management (mainly budgeting).

Building a new department is a one-off opportunity to establish good accounting processes without being hindered by too many existing financial obstacles. Use the ITIL Financial Management component as described in the ITIL v3 publication *Service Strategy* as your guide.

Communicating with peers and customers

Communicating at all levels is the very lifeblood of IT Service Management, because it handles the vast majority of contact with the customers. When building an IT Service Management department you have to review the communication paths and content for every function, activity and process, whether they flow internally or externally. Create a standard 'look and feel' for all Service Management communications, e.g. for presentation templates, typefaces and colours etc., so that all IT Service Management communications on paper or on screen are instantly recognizable. In a larger IT Service Management department you may want to appoint a Communications Standards Officer who will create and register the format of all regular communications, e.g. incident reports. Any complaints or concerns about communications should be registered and treated as an incident.

Developing and producing technologies and systems

Here we are talking exclusively of the technologies and systems required to run IT Service Management, including hardware, software and telecommunications. This should be a centralized service to cover all Service Management technology requirements, and should also be attached to all other development projects producing services that will affect or involve Service Management services or technologies. It should cover all stages of developing and producing technologies, from feasibility to installation. It may not be possible to handle these activities within small Service Management departments, in which case you should still allocate a Service Management representative who will work with the external resources.

Performing operational activities

The main activities are explained in the ITIL v3 publication *Service Operation*. The Service Operation roles may be distributed throughout Service Management, from the Service Desk to network operators. Make sure that you read and fully understand the lessons in *Service Operation*.

Performing key basic support tasks

There are always many basic tasks, such as local database management, that are not performed correctly, because the responsibilities for these tasks are not correctly allocated. Avoid the danger of forgetting those basic tasks when creating your department.

The pyramid approach is useful because it puts into perspective the functions required for a successful department. If we look at a summary of the structure, the picture becomes clearer. In Figure 1.5 the eight levels are easy to follow, but you must not make the mistake of thinking that departmental functions and processes may reside on only one level. The Service Desk is an example of a function that can reside on more than one level.

Figure 1.5 Service Management department structure

Many Service Desks operate at the levels illustrated in Figure 1.6, with a front end handling the simple incidents, and a more skilled and qualified level to handle the more complex incidents. In addition, many Service Desks are used to communicate information to the customers – for example, notification of planned system outages. It is not intended that you try to construct a Service Management department based strictly on these levels, but that you understand that any successful department needs to incorporate all the functions that relate to these levels.

These levels are not necessarily represented by an organization chart because organization charts are more concerned with reporting levels than functions and their relationships. For example, staff operating at a higher level would not necessarily be better graded or earn more money because they are contributing to a different stratum on the pyramid. The key is to

Figure 1.6 Multi-level Service Desk

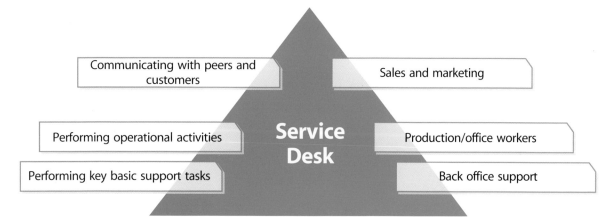

consider all the points listed in Figure 1.5 and ensure that your department encompasses all of them. You could change the list in Figure 1.5 to a set of questions that you would pose for every function (i.e. process or activity) such as Service Desk or Change Management:

1. Is this function within the scope as described by **the focal point, the pinnacle or the mission**?
2. Are there any **key decisions** to be made when performing this function?
3. How will this function **put its decisions into practice**?
4. How will this function manage its **documentation and finances**?
5. How does this function **communicate with its peers and customers**?
6. Who will **develop and produce the technologies and systems** required by this function?
7. Will this function be **performing any operational activities** and, if so, how are the actions performed?
8. Is this function responsible for **performing key basic tasks** and, if so, how are those tasks performed?

In the above list, each of the different levels from Figure 1.5 is shown in bold. You should ask these questions for every function as you include it, or consider including it, in your Service Management department, and then take any necessary action that may be required as a result. This will ensure that your new department will be well balanced and seamlessly integrated.

Overview of a step-by-step approach

2 Overview of a step-by-step approach

2.1 WHY A STEP-BY-STEP APPROACH?

This publication is intended as a practical guide to assist IT Service Management professionals to build a successful Service Management department. A project-based step-by-step approach was selected, as this matches the way that Service Management professionals think.

2.2 THE STEPS

There are nine sequential steps described in this publication, which plot the path to building a successful Service Management department. These steps could easily be converted into a project if required.

Figure 2.1 The steps to success

1. Preparing the basics
2. Defining departmental parameters
3. Identifying primary ITIL Fundamental Tasks
4. Identifying non-ITIL Fundamental Tasks
5. Rationalizing the Fundamental Tasks
6. Creating Associated Fundamental Task Packs
7. Constructing your Service Management department
8. Organizational plans and charts
9. Resourcing your Service Management department

As you can see in Figure 2.1, the steps link together logically to form a cohesive plan. However, this may be better explained by looking at a quick overview (each step is covered in a separate chapter in this publication).

Step 1 – Preparing the basics

The basics included in this step are:

- How to adopt a project approach
- Selecting a team to work on building the department
- Collating existing materials, e.g. organization charts
- Linking into any existing ITIL implementations that may be under way.

Step 2 – Defining departmental parameters

To create a successful Service Management department, direction and structure both need to be established very early in the project. This step has two main components – the creation of a mission statement, and then a set of parameters to deliver that mission statement. There is an example of a mission statement (or goals) in Chapter 4 plus a set of parameters including:

- The ITIL processes, activities and functions should remain as efficient and as intact as possible.
- Other best-practice processes, activities and functions should remain as efficient and as intact as possible.
- The department must meet all governance and legislation requirements.

This is a crucial step because the mission statement and its accompanying parameters will ensure that the project will stay on course and that all parties fully understand the deliverables.

Step 3 – Identifying primary ITIL Fundamental Tasks

This step includes defining, identifying and documenting the primary ITIL Fundamental Tasks (FTs) to include in your department.

ITIL Fundamental Tasks are the activities and process as stipulated by ITIL, e.g. Service Desk Incident Management, Problem Management, Event Management and Change Management. In a small department these could be tasks performed by an individual, whereas in a larger department they could be handled by teams of people, but either way they are valid tasks.

Step 4 – Identifying non-ITIL Fundamental Tasks

This step is in some ways similar to the previous steps, except that it acknowledges that not all of the Fundamental Tasks required by a Service Management department can be found in ITIL publications – for example, Process Design, Human Resourcing and Education. The objective is to identify any non-ITIL Fundamental Tasks required to run your Service Management department.

Step 5 – Rationalizing the Fundamental Tasks

This step is primarily concerned with categorizing the Fundamental Tasks identified so far into three categories – Current Fundamental Tasks, Planned Fundamental Tasks and Rejected Fundamental Tasks. Obviously we can remove the Rejected Fundamental Tasks at this stage. We must remember to review our departmental parameters because a mistake here could cause problems later in the project.

Step 6 – Creating Associated Fundamental Task Packs

A Service Management department cannot be created from a set of disparate Fundamental Tasks. You may have 30 or more Fundamental Tasks, and it will take too long and become very confusing. This step removes this problem by explaining how to group the Fundamental Tasks into smaller Associated Fundamental Task Packs (AFTPs). After defining an Associated Fundamental Task Pack, the step also involves:

- Benefits of Associated Fundamental Task Packs
- Establishing Associated Fundamental Task Packs
- Meeting the departmental parameters
- Documenting the Associated Fundamental Task Packs.

Step 7 – Constructing your Service Management department

This is where the planning and construction is undertaken so that organizational plans and charts can be prepared.

Step 8 – Organizational plans and charts

Organizational charts are used in almost every organization. They are discussed here to ensure that our new department can be understood by management and customers.

Step 9 – Resourcing your Service Management department

With all of the construction now complete, it is time to provide the resources for your Service Management department, including job descriptions, processes and work instructions and Service Management technology.

For a more comprehensive plan, please refer to Chapter 12.

Step 1 – Preparing the basics

3 Step 1 – Preparing the basics

3.1 A PROJECT APPROACH

Constructing or rebuilding a Service Management department is a major exercise that will involve the rest of IT and, of course, the Service Management customers. It is not the kind of exercise where you can experiment, because at all times the needs and demands of the Service Management customers must come first. There will be some effect on the customers due to changes of structure and reporting, but these should not have a negative effect on Service Management performance if careful planning is employed. This is why project management is so important.

Many projects are of a linear nature: they start with a charter and then progress through a series of steps until they reach the desired outcome – for example, the development of a new system or service. This project would differ because many of the steps would need to be repeated for each function – for example, you need to repeat the steps required to create a function description.

Figure 3.1 shows an example of a repetitive step group, where the five steps highlighted would be repeated for every function. For example, if you were working on Incident, Problem and Change, you would repeat these steps for each of these functions. Other steps such as creating a departmental mission statement would not be repeated.

The advantage of repetitive step groups is that they allow numerous functions to be worked on simultaneously. When building your project you should construct repetitive step groups to improve the efficiency of your project.

A good tip is to adopt a project-management best practice, such as PRINCE2™, to help you design a better project.

3.2 SELECTING A PROJECT TEAM

Obviously, the success of a project depends on the team selected to work on it. However, even the best team can struggle if the members have been selected for

Figure 3.1 Repetitive step group

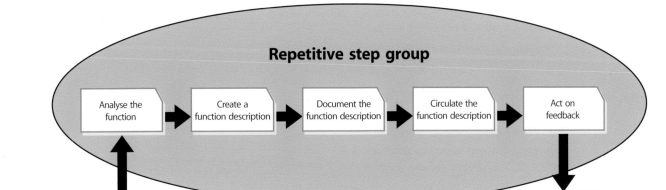

the wrong reasons so you may want to use a project discipline such as PRINCE2, which helps to design and manage projects. Typically, this type of project should draw the project team from three different resource pools:

- **Permanent project team members** These are the people who have been assigned to the project for the whole duration, or for a large part of it. Ideally, there would be at least three skill sets among the permanent team members – ITIL awareness, Service Management experience and departmental construction knowledge. The hardest of these skill sets to bring to the team is departmental construction knowledge – such experience is rare and is not likely to reside within IT. If departmental construction knowledge, or any of the skill sets, cannot be attached to the project, then the project team members must ensure that they educate themselves to replace the missing skills.

- **Supplementary project team members** In a project of this nature, it is inevitable that some specialist skills will be required for small portions of the project. It is therefore a good idea to identify as many of these as possible at the project-planning stage so that you can discuss your potential requirements with the appropriate managers. You will get more cooperation if you discuss this with managers at the start of your project rather than waiting until you need the skills.

- **Project advisers** Although these people will not be active project members, they can still provide a valuable role in advising and guiding the project. Project advisers could include human resources staff, corporate auditors, financial planners and governance officers. It is better to involve these people as advisers than have them demanding changes to your department at the end of your project. You should consult them at regular intervals throughout the project.

It is also likely that you will have a Project Advisory Board to direct and guide your project. Do not underestimate the need for a project approach both for the success of the project and for the credibility that you will get from other IT departments, such as Development.

3.3 COLLATING CURRENT MATERIALS

One of the first tasks that you should undertake is to collate all the documentation relating to the existing Service Management department or functions. This includes items such as organization charts, job descriptions, work instructions and process documentation. The idea is to familiarize yourself with the current situation, while at the same time deciding which documentation will be useful later in the project.

3.4 OTHER ITIL PROJECTS

If you are starting a project to implement a Service Management department based around ITIL, then it is highly likely that there is at least one other ITIL project under construction in your organization. You should identify these schemes and work together to align your respective projects. For example, there may be a plan in place to install improved Change Management, in which case you may want to work on the staffing side as soon as possible.

Step 2 – Defining departmental parameters

4

4 Step 2 – Defining departmental parameters

4.1 CREATING A MISSION STATEMENT

The most successful mission statements are those created in consultation with those who may be directly affected by the new department (e.g. those already performing Service Management tasks), potential Service Management customers and senior management. Consulting these people is important because it helps broaden your horizons and gain some insight into people's vision of the new Service Management department. Having a mission statement is important in order to remove any confusion or misconceptions concerning the new department. Not everyone will agree with the mission statement, but they will understand it and know what to expect.

Mission statements must be clear, and the best are usually brief – between one and three sentences. The more you digress the more difficult the project can be to manage. Your mission statement should be easily understood by team members and all of the people who were consulted before creating it.

Here is an example of a mission statement:

> To create a Service Management department from the activities, functions and processes described and defined by the ITIL best practices and any other industry-related best practices such as the Control Objectives for Information and related Technology (COBIT – www.isaca.org). The department must conform to all governance and legislation requirements.

The statement is concise but clear, and when we add the parameters the deliverables will have more clarity.

4.2 INTRODUCTION TO DEPARTMENTAL PARAMETERS

It is important to have a set of parameters that will guide and focus the development and creation phases, while ensuring that the mission statement will be delivered. Often the deliverables of a project differ from the expected result, because projects go through an evolution process as they progress. This is why it is so important to have some parameters to harness the project team. These parameters are often called 'terms of reference' or the project 'charter'. They should focus decision-making within the project and ensure that the end product meets expectations, without unduly hindering the progression of the project.

Before we can review some suggested parameters, it is important to have a brief overview of Fundamental Tasks (FTs) and Associated Fundamental Task Packs (AFTPs). (These will be covered in more detail in later chapters.)

4.2.1 Fundamental Tasks

These are the processes, functions and activities that have to be performed to provide Service Management to IT customers – e.g. Service Desk, Incident Management, Event Management and Problem Management are all Fundamental Tasks. There are over 30 Fundamental Tasks described in ITIL v3; these will be discussed in later chapters.

4.2.2 Associated Fundamental Task Packs

These are groups of Fundamental Tasks that work together as a cohesive unit.

Figure 4.1 Example of an Associated Fundamental Task Pack

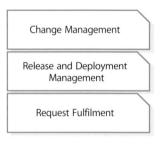

Figure 4.1 illustrates Fundamental Tasks that fit together neatly to make an Associated Fundamental Task Pack.

We can use ITIL and other resources to identify our Fundamental Tasks, but the Associated Fundamental Task Packs are unique to each Service Management department.

4.3 CREATING THE PARAMETERS

Once you have created your mission statement, you need to identify the parameters that will ensure that your completed Service Management department delivers that mission statement. It is important that the parameters are established before any identification of Fundamental Tasks begins, since the nature of the parameters will influence how you identify and select your Fundamental Tasks. The following is a list of suggested parameters from which you can create your own departmental parameters.

- The ITIL processes, activities and functions should remain as efficient and as intact as possible. The intention is to create a Service Management department following the ITIL guidelines; this statement may therefore seem a little superfluous, but it is important to include it because the project should not wander from the ITIL path without identifying the deviation and approving the new direction. Each of the ITIL processes, activities and functions is clearly identified in the ITIL v3 and v2 publications, so it should be easy to follow this parameter. This parameter will govern the selection of Fundamental Tasks.
- Other best-practice processes, activities and functions should remain as efficient and as intact as possible – most Service Management departments are subject to more best practices than just ITIL – for example COBIT. Many of these may have their own processes, activities and functions in addition to those defined by ITIL, so this is an important parameter to include. Not all of these extra processes, activities and functions are as clearly defined as they are in ITIL, so this parameter could include a statement that if they are not described in the best practice, they should be documented as part of building your Service Management department. This parameter will govern the extent of the inclusion of other best practices within the Service Management department.
- The department must meet all governance and legislation requirements. This parameter is similar to the previous two, except that many of the criteria required to meet governance and legislation are not negotiable. The concept is to create a Service Management department that is conformant with legislation and governance. Therefore, it is important to involve experts from these areas throughout the creation of your Service Management department, to ensure that there are no nasty surprises when you build your department or, even worse, at the end of your project.
- The scope of the Fundamental Tasks should encompass more than the ITIL Service Management processes. Not all of the processes, activities and functions required to run a department can be found in ITIL or other best-practice publications – for example, Human Resources, Education and Process Engineering. This parameter is important so that when selecting your Fundamental Tasks you do not ignore, or forget, any other processes, activities and functions.

- Each Fundamental Task must either be ITIL-conformant or contribute towards meeting the ITIL goals and benefits. The most important factor of this parameter is that the ITIL goals and benefits are regularly reviewed as part of the department build process. You may, of course, add your own goals and benefits to supplement those suggested by ITIL.
- Fundamental Tasks must connect or integrate together logically within an Associated Fundamental Task Pack. Ideally, the Fundamental Tasks within an AFTP should entail similar skill sets, technology resources and common or similar metrics. This parameter is to ensure fluidity in your new Service Management department by ensuring a logical grouping of Fundamental Tasks (see Figure 4.2).

Figure 4.2 Logical grouping of Fundamental Tasks

The idea is to create Associated Fundamental Task Packs that are self-sufficient but that contribute fully to the new Service Management department. If we take the criterion of skill sets from the previous bullet point, it is easy to see how the staff working in the Associated Fundamental Task Pack shown in Figure 4.2 would have similar and complementary skill sets, and when it comes to technology resources one tool should include all, or most, of these functions. It is also easy to see how common or similar metrics could be applied. This is an important parameter, because poorly designed AFTPs will cause duplication, confrontation and confusion.

- The Fundamental Tasks within an Associated Fundamental Task Pack should collectively provide a focused level of joint responsibility. This parameter could be added as another component of the previous parameter; however, because it is so important it is worth having a parameter all to itself. Nothing focuses a unit in a department more than joint responsibility, i.e. we are all responsible as a team for the consequences of our actions. This is an important parameter when combining Fundamental Tasks into Associated Fundamental Task Packs.
- The Fundamental Tasks in an Associated Fundamental Task Pack should have a common personality. This is about the staffing mix contained with the various groups in a department. For example, Service Desk staff are usually outgoing and are good communicators, whereas network designers are happier in a quieter environment, working alone; this makes it difficult to unite these two roles into the same Associated Fundamental Task Pack. So this parameter is here to ensure that staff relationships are considered regularly when constructing a Service Management department.

The parameters included here are meant as a guide – you may decide not to include some of them or to add some that relate to your Service Management requirements. Either way, it is important that you create parameters to focus the planning and construction of your Service Management department.

Finally you should document your mission statement and parameters for publication and distribution. The following chart (Figure 4.3) is a good way to illustrate the mission statement and its supporting parameters.

Figure 4.3 Example of a mission statement chart

Goals or mission statement

To create a Service Management department from the activities, functions and processes described and defined by the ITIL best practices and any other relevant best practices that have been approved by management. The department must conform to all governance and legislation requirements.

Parameters

- The ITIL processes, activities and functions should remain as efficient and as intact as possible
- Other best practice processes, activities and functions should remain as efficient and as intact as possible
- The department must meet all governance and legislation requirements
- The scope of the Fundamental Tasks should encompass more than the ITIL Service Management processes
- Each Fundamental Task must be either ITIL-compliant or contribute towards meeting the ITIL goals and benefits
- Fundamental Tasks (FTs) must connect or integrate together logically within an Associated Fundamental Task Pack (AFTP); ideally, the Fundamental Tasks within an Associated Fundamental Task Pack should entail similar skill sets, technology resources and common or similar metrics
- The Fundamental Tasks within an Associated Fundamental Task Pack should collectively provide a focused level of joint responsibility
- The Fundamental Tasks in an Associated Fundamental Task Pack should have a common personality

When you distribute your mission statement and parameters, make sure that you request feedback so that you can review any possible amendments and identify and deal with any potential contentious issues before they arise.

Step 3 – Identifying primary ITIL Fundamental Tasks

5 Step 3 – Identifying primary ITIL Fundamental Tasks

5.1 DEFINITION OF THE PRIMARY ITIL FUNDAMENTAL TASKS

It is now time to collate a list of the ITIL activities, functions and processes, but at this point without deciding whether they are going to be included in your Service Management department. The idea is to create a list for discussion and consideration. Be sure to include all relevant ITIL v3 materials (or v2 materials if you prefer this version of ITIL) because at this point you need to stay unbiased and concentrate on the bigger picture. Even if you are not an ITIL shop, you can use the ITIL processes, functions and activities as a useful guide.

Each of the processes, functions and activities will be classified as a Fundamental Task. The definition of a Fundamental Task is:

> A function, activity or process that can be performed as an independent activity even if it depends upon input from other Fundamental Tasks and/or provides output that becomes input to another Fundamental Task. It should be possible for the Fundamental Tasks to have targets and objectives.

To fully understand the Fundamental Task definition it is important we that we understand the definition of processes, functions and activities. To help us to understand them better the following quotes have been extracted from the ITIL glossary:

> **Function** A team or group of people and the tools they use to carry out one or more processes or activities. For example, the Service Desk.
>
> **Activity** A set of actions designed to achieve a particular result. Activities are usually defined as part of processes or plans and are documented in procedures. For example, the escalation of an incident is an activity.
>
> **Process** A structured set of activities designed to accomplish a specific objective. A process takes one or more defined inputs and turns them into defined outputs. For example, you could build a process to perform Incident Management.

A common scenario is a good way to better understand these definitions: for example a function called the Service Desk being responsible for two prime processes known as Incident and Problem Management and, while applying these processes, performing a series of activities such as incident escalation and problem logging.

It is important to keep in mind that these are tasks and not jobs. For example, in a small organization one person may perform Incident Management, Change Management and Problem Management in a morning, whereas in a large organization these same tasks may require the dedicated efforts of many people on a 24/7 basis.

Many organizations have already identified numerous Fundamental Tasks without seeing ITIL, because Fundamental Tasks are often obvious. For example every Help or Service Desk is already performing Incident Management even though they may not be following the prescribed ITIL guidelines for Incident Management, whereas with Change

Management every organization performs changes but not many manage them. The concept here is to identify potential Fundamental Tasks whether they are being performed at the moment or not.

5.2 IDENTIFYING THE ITIL FUNDAMENTAL TASKS

The best way to approach this exercise is to review each of the five core ITIL version 3 publications to identify and log each of the Fundamental Tasks. The Fundamental Tasks have the label 'primary' because they are the highest-level tasks, and in fact some of these Fundamental Tasks contain sub-processes. These primary Fundamental Tasks have been selected because they appear in the table of contents in the ITIL v3 publications.

Identifying the Fundamental Tasks can be made much more effective and efficient if some of the staff involved in this project have some ITIL certified training. The best approach is to work systematically through the ITIL publications identifying the Fundamental Tasks.

Figure 5.1 includes the majority of the ITIL version 3 Fundamental Tasks. These are listed under the titles of their associated ITIL v3 publications. It is highly likely that you will find some more, because there will always be some small disputes, even among experts, as to whether some items should be classified as functions, activities or processes. This should not affect your role here, which is to identify without prejudice all of the ITIL Fundamental Tasks – so, if in doubt, include a task in your list.

Figure 5.1 ITIL v3 Fundamental Tasks

Service Strategy	Service Design	Service Operation	Service Transition	Continual Service Improvement
Financial Management	Service Catalogue Management	Event Management	Transitional Planning and Support	The 7-Step Improvement Process
Service Portfolio Management	Service Level Management	Incident Management	Change Management	Service Reporting
Demand Management	Capacity Management	Request Fulfilment	Service Asset and Configuration Management	Service Measurement
	Availability Management	Problem Management	Release and Deployment Management	Return on Investment for CSI
	IT Service Continuity Management	Access Management	Service Validation and Testing	Business Questions for CSI
	Information Security Management	Operational Activities in other Lifecycle Phases	Evaluation	
	Supplier Management	Service Desk	Knowledge Management	
	Requirements Engineering	Technical Management		
	Data and Information Management	IT Operations Management (Control and Facilities)		
		Applications Management		

To prepare your list of Fundamental Tasks you should look at each of the Fundamental Tasks that you identify and ask whether you would like to include it in your Service Management department. It doesn't matter here whether you are already performing all these Fundamental Tasks or not; include all Fundamental Tasks that you have chosen at this point because you are identifying the 'potential' FTs for your SM department. It is quite possible that some of the Fundamental Tasks that you select here may be removed later, for example if senior management decide that a particular FT should reside elsewhere.

Some selections can be confusing. For example, Capacity Management activities may be performed at various locations depending upon different technology components, which would suggest that this Fundamental Task may reside elsewhere. But if end-to-end Capacity Management is to be performed for a service rather than just for a technology component, then Capacity Management will need to reside in one location so that all of the components required for a service can be orchestrated to provide overall Capacity Management. So when considering your Fundamental Tasks keep in mind that not all of the activities will be performed by Service Management. At this stage do not get confused; if in doubt include the Fundamental Task in your list and press on with preparing your list.

At this point you should have your list of ITIL Fundamental Tasks for consideration for your Service Management department.

5.3 DOCUMENTING THE ITIL FUNDAMENTAL TASKS

The Fundamental Tasks vary widely and do not naturally fit together as a snug department. Each of the functions, activities and processes in Figure 5.1 qualifies as a Fundamental Task and needs to be included in your list. If you find any others, they should be added to the list.

As you identify the functions, processes and activities, you need to create brief descriptions so that people who are not conversant with ITIL can understand the potential of each. ITIL is meant to be flexible, so it is also possible that you are performing some of the tasks, but not in exactly the same way as described in ITIL. It is therefore important that you enter the description of your processes rather than the definition used in the ITIL publication.

You should document your list so that it can be circulated for comments and suggestions. There is no point circulating a simple list of Fundamental Task names – you will need to provide a brief description of each Fundamental Task. A simple spreadsheet is a good way to document your Fundamental Tasks ready for distribution and evaluation.

The example in Figure 5.2 is Incident Management. This has been chosen because without knowing the definition of an incident, is it is impossible to understand the definition of Incident Management, which is why the description of an incident has been included in the 'Definition' column. Following Figure 5.2 from left to right, we start with the name of the ITIL Fundamental Task, followed by the ITIL publication, or publications, where more information concerning the FT can be found if required. Next is the definition, where the Fundamental Task definition is in normal typeface, and any additional definition is in italics.

The definition of Incident Management is from the ITIL glossary. However, if you are currently performing a Fundamental Task but are not using the ITIL definition, you may want to put in here the description of how you are performing this Fundamental Task at the moment. Finally, the last column shows whether this Fundamental Task is currently active in your organization – if it is not currently active then 'Not applicable' could be inserted here. This is a lot of information, but in a format that is easy to create and follow.

Step 3 – Identifying primary ITIL Fundamental Tasks

Figure 5.2 Example of Fundamental Task documentation

Fundamental Task	ITIL publication	Definition	Current owner
Incident Management	Service Operation	The process responsible for managing the life-cycle of all incidents. The primary objective of Incident Management is to return the IT service to customers as quickly as possible *Definition of an incident – an unplanned interruption of an IT service or reduction in the quality of an IT service. Failure of a Configuration Item that has not yet affected service is also an incident. For example, the failure of a disk from a mirror set.*	Service Support section

At the end of this stage, you should have identified and documented all the potential Fundamental Tasks included in the ITIL publications. At this point you should distribute your Fundamental Task descriptions, making sure that you request feedback so that you can review any possible amendments, and identify and deal with any potential contentious issues before they arise.

Step 4 – Identifying non-ITIL Fundamental Tasks

6 Step 4 – Identifying non-ITIL Fundamental Tasks

6.1 DEFINITION OF A NON-ITIL FUNDAMENTAL TASK

ITIL does not contain all departmental tasks, but concentrates on those required to manage Service Management. We will be using two definitions here to explain how to identify non-ITIL tasks:

- Tasks not included in the ITIL publications – a good example would be Human Resource Management, particularly in the arena of training, education and certification. This has to be planned, justified and managed. In addition, there are all the other HR tasks such as counselling, recruitment, job descriptions and staff evaluations. In smaller Service Management departments this could be quite a small task, but in a larger department it could involve a team of people.
- Tasks included in ITIL but at a low level – as mentioned earlier, some tasks and processes are included as a subset of higher-level Fundamental Tasks. Contract Management is a good example; it is mentioned in four of the ITIL v3 publications and is a key component of a well-run Service Management department. Therefore it could easily qualify as a Fundamental Task.

The tasks not included in ITIL are often apparent, but only by reading the ITIL publications and obtaining some ITIL education will you be able to spot the sub-tasks within the ITIL framework.

6.2 EXAMPLES OF NON-ITIL FUNDAMENTAL TASKS

It is impossible to identify the non-ITIL Fundamental Tasks here – there could be many tasks, depending on how you are approaching the task of building your ITIL Service Management department. However, to help you with this project, here are some examples.

Figure 6.1 Non-ITIL Fundamental Tasks

Low-level ITIL tasks

- Business Service Management
- SM Governance Management
- Contract Management
- Business Relationship Management

Additional tasks

- Process Design and Management
- HR and Education

In Figure 6.1 we have identified six non-ITIL tasks to be included in the prototype Service Management departments, which will be explored in later chapters. The first four tasks are spread among the ITIL publications, but not with any prominence, which is why they are included here. Remember that these are only tasks and not jobs, so that even in smaller Service Management departments you may have an SM contract manager, even if it is not a full-time job. The last two additional tasks do not have any prominence in the ITIL publications because they are administrative tasks. This does not make them less important – for example, some of the ITIL implementation failures have been due to lack of process-engineering skills.

It is highly unlikely that you will include all six tasks in your Service Management department, because the selection and identification of these tasks is highly subjective. Now we have 40 Fundamental Tasks, as shown in Figure 6.2.

Figure 6.2 may look daunting, but remember this is the complete list, and in the next step we will eliminate those Fundamental Tasks that are not required in our department. For ease of reference, in Figure 6.2 the ITIL Fundamental Tasks are in italics. The idea has been to create a list without prejudice – in other words, without making arbitrary decisions to eliminate some tasks without consulting with the rest of IT and management. It is also a good way to alert the rest of IT to the scale and scope of the activities performed by Service Management.

Figure 6.2 ITIL v3 and non-ITIL Fundamental Tasks

Service Strategy	Service Design	Service Operation	Service Transition	Continual Service Improvement
Financial Management	*Service Catalogue Management*	*Event Management*	*Transitional Planning and Support*	*The 7-Step Improvement Process*
Service Portfolio Management	*Service Level Management*	*Incident Management*	*Change Management*	*Service Reporting*
Demand Management	*Capacity Management*	*Request Fulfilment*	*Service Asset and Configuration Management*	*Service Measurement*
Business Service Management	*Availability Management*	*Problem Management*	*Release and Deployment Management*	*Return on Investment for CSI*
SM Governance Management	*IT Service Continuity Management*	*Access Management*	*Service Validation and Testing*	*Business Questions for CSI*
HR and Education	*Information Security Management*	*Operational Activities in other Lifecycle Phases*	*Evaluation*	
Contract Management	*Supplier Management*	*Service Desk*	*Knowledge Management*	
	Requirements Engineering	*Technical Management*		
	Data and Information Management	*IT Operations Management (Control and Facilities)*		
	Business Relationship Management	*Applications Management*		
	Process Design and Management			

6.3 PREPARING TO LOCATE NON-ITIL FUNDAMENTAL TASKS

Success depends on good planning and preparation, so do not skimp on this. Identifying non-ITIL Fundamental tasks is more challenging than identifying primary ITIL Fundamental Tasks, because the information needs to be collated from a far wider source. Here are some of the sources.

6.3.1 Education

ITIL knowledge is important for this project – the higher the level of knowledge, the better.

6.3.2 Conferences and seminars

Networking is a prime source of learning and should not be ignored. The tip is not how many conferences and seminars you attend, but the preparation before you attend and sharing the lessons learned when you return. You should:

- Prepare a checklist of questions before attending so that you can focus networking.
- Have different checklists if more than one of the project team is attending.
- Carefully select which sessions to attend and make notes of any relevant points during the session.
- Approach presenters if you have any questions or concerns.
- Document all the information you have obtained from conferences and seminars; make sure that all of the team document their findings and use the same format so that you can store this knowledge as a consistent reference resource.
- Ensure that each team member debriefs the rest of the team with the information that they have collated.

This can all be summed up in the phrase 'prepare, attend and debrief' (PAD).

Don't be shy to attend vendor events – they are free and have some great guest speakers.

6.3.3 Institutes and local interest groups

Industry associations are a good source of information and inspiration. Join and attend as many meetings as you can, and remember to use the PAD approach. Also check out the groups' publications and bookstores.

6.3.4 ITIL v2 and v3 publications

Delve into ITIL v2 and v3 publications to identify and review the ITIL sub-tasks and determine whether they should become Fundamental Tasks. You can perform this activity at the same time that you review ITIL for the Fundamental Tasks. Another good source is the ITIL glossary, as many of the sub-tasks are described there with references to the publications in which they figure.

6.3.5 Experts

Delving into the ITIL publications, although an important exercise, can be time-consuming. It is therefore a good idea to consult with ITIL experts to help pinpoint some of the less apparent tasks.

Keep in mind that the project is to build a department and not to implement ITIL, so consider consulting experts on specifying and building departments. Contact your human resources department – they may be able to help locate the necessary experts.

6.4 IDENTIFYING THE NON-ITIL FUNDAMENTAL TASKS

It is highly likely that you will identify some non-ITIL Fundamental Tasks while performing your planning and preparation, in which case you should document these as you identify them. With the correct preparation, identifying the non-ITIL Fundamental Tasks should not be difficult. However, there are some significant factors that can help focus your efforts.

- **Service Management staff** Have you ever met a Service Desk agent who doesn't have an opinion on almost everything? No? Well don't waste this valuable resource. Discuss your objectives with current Service Management staff and ask for their input, ideas and suggestions. Your Service Management staff may not all be reporting to the same source at the moment – for example, the Service Desk and Change Management may report to different managers – so the best approach is to identify the staff who are performing any of the ITIL Fundamental Tasks that you have previously identified and interview them.
- **Customers** The main reason for building a Service Management department is to improve the levels of service that customers receive from IT. Therefore, customers are an obvious source to be interviewed. Primarily, you are asking customers for their ideas and suggestions to improve the IT service, and from this you should be able to identify any potential non-ITIL Fundamental Tasks. Again it is a case of applying the PAD methodology.
- **The rest of IT** If we are to improve the service levels for the customer, then the rest of IT must be involved – without their contribution it is very difficult to make a significant improvement in service levels. You will need to identify those IT departments that are closest to Service Management, discuss your objectives with them and ask for their input, ideas and suggestions. Once again, apply the PAD methodology.
- **Look at current tasks** It is possible that some non-ITIL Fundamental Tasks are performed at the moment in your Service Management function. Therefore, you should review how Service Management is currently performed in your organization to see if you can identify any non-ITIL Fundamental Tasks currently in use.
- **Current problems and issues** You may have some current Service Management issues, e.g. inability to meet availability targets. If this is the case, try to determine whether the introduction of a non-ITIL Fundamental Task could help solve the situation – and don't ignore the fact that an ITIL Fundamental Task may be the solution.
- **Look at what is missing** Sometimes it is a case of something missing rather than something wrong. For example, is your Service Management team performing manual tasks to complete an activity? Or maybe they have inadequate and slow technology. The missing component may well be an ITIL non-Fundamental Task, but in some cases it could be a non-ITIL Fundamental Task. Review your current Service Management activities for gaps and weaknesses.
- **Future planning** You may be coping adequately at the moment, but do you have the tasks in place for the new systems and services in the pipeline? Here you should identify all services and systems that are in development or planning and try to determine whether they will need any non-ITIL Fundamental Tasks to be implemented.

Remember: do not eliminate any non-ITIL Fundamental Tasks at this stage, because the objective is to keep an open mind to ensure that no tasks are prematurely eliminated.

By now you should have identified and collated your non-ITIL Fundamental Tasks ready for the next step, which is to document them.

6.5 DOCUMENTING NON-ITIL TASKS

Documenting non-ITIL Fundamental Tasks follows the same method as described in the previous chapter. To illustrate this point, the six tasks contained in Figure 6.1 are described in Table 6.1, using the same format as in Figure 5.2, Example of Fundamental Task documentation.

Table 6.1 ITIL v3 and non-ITIL Fundamental Tasks

Fundamental Task	ITIL publication	Definition	Current owner
Business Service Management	Service Strategy and Design	An approach to the management of IT Services that considers the business processes supported and the business value provided.	Not performed at present
		■ Align IT service provision with business goals and objectives.	
		■ Prioritize all IT activities and business impact and urgency, ensuring critical business processes and services receive the most attention.	
		■ Increase business productivity and profitability through the increased efficiency and effectiveness of IT processes.	
		■ Support the requirements to corporate governance with appropriate IT governance and controls.	
		■ Create competitive advantage through the exploitation and innovation of IT infrastructure as a whole.	
		■ Improve service quality, customer satisfaction, user perception and innovation of IT infrastructure as a whole.	
		■ Ensure regulatory and legislative compliance.	
		■ Ensure appropriate levels of protection on all IT and information assets.	
		■ Ensure that IT services are aligned and continue to be aligned with changing business needs.	
Governance Management	Continual Service Improvement and Service Strategy	Ensuring that policies and strategy are actually implemented, and that required processes are correctly followed. Governance includes defining roles and responsibilities, measuring and reporting, and taking actions to resolve any issues identified.	Spread around IT units
		Governance Management must keep abreast of all changes and updates to any governance that affects Service Management and ensure that any amendments are performed in a timely manner so that conformance with SM governance remains intact.	
		Governance Management should check all changes to ensure that governance conformance is not broken due to a change.	
		Governance Management will perform occasional due diligence to ensure that SM conforms to governance requirements.	

Step 4 – Identifying non-ITIL Fundamental Tasks

Table 6.1 *continued*

Fundamental Task	ITIL publication	Definition	Current owner
Contract Management	Service Strategy, Service Operation and Service Design	Responsible for ensuring that all contracts relating to IT Service Management are maintained, relevant and adhered to. This includes ensuring that there are no duplicate contracts and that all contracts are in operation (e.g. not paying for software contracts for old redundant software). Would also be involved in identifying basic contract contents, contract evaluations, formal contracts, renewal/termination and underpinning contracts. Work closely with corporate contract management and purchasing departments.	Spread around IT units
Business Relationship Management	Service Strategy, Service Design and Continual Service Improvement	The process or function responsible for maintaining a relationship with the business. Business Relationship Management includes: ■ Managing personal relationships with business managers ■ Providing input to Service Portfolio Management ■ Ensuring that the IT service provider is satisfying the business needs of the customers ■ Reviewing all relevant metrics with customers ■ Providing the customers with independent support during outages and failures. Business relationship managers are to meet regularly with their customers to ensure an on-going relationship with IT, improve understanding and promote harmony.	Not performed at present
Process Design and Management	N/A	Process Management is an independent unit responsible for: ■ Process design ■ Process construction ■ Process implementation ■ Process documentation ■ Ensuring that processes remain fit for purpose ■ Monitoring the effectiveness of processes ■ Contributing to the automation of processes ■ Contributing to Change Management ensuring the integrity of the SM processes ■ Integration between processes.	Units are responsible for their own processes

Step 4 – Identifying non-ITIL Fundamental Tasks

Fundamental Task	ITIL publication	Definition	Current owner
HR and Education	N/A	Responsible for Service Management HR activities including: ■ Counselling ■ Recruitment ■ Job descriptions ■ Staff evaluations ■ Education planning and management ■ Certification.	Corporate HR handles some of the tasks

At the end of this stage, you should have identified and documented any potential non-ITIL Fundamental Tasks. At this point you should distribute your non-ITIL Fundamental Task descriptions, making sure that you request feedback so that you can review any possible amendments and identify and deal with any potential contentious issues before they arise.

Step 5 – Rationalizing the Fundamental Tasks

7 Step 5 – Rationalizing the Fundamental Tasks

In the previous two chapters we have discussed how to identify the ITIL and non-ITIL Fundamental Tasks, without eliminating any of them and without identifying those Fundamental Tasks that are already being performed by your Service Management team.

7.1 RATING THE TASKS

In order to rationalize the Fundamental Tasks, we now need to rate each of them so that our task list can be redrawn.

7.1.1 Current Fundamental Tasks

These are the Fundamental Tasks that are currently being performed within IT, though not necessarily at the moment by Service Management – for example, Capacity Management may be performed by a technical team or department.

7.1.2 Planned Fundamental Tasks

These are the Fundamental Tasks that are not yet in place but are planned to be implemented as they are developed. The concept here is to create an environment to allow these new Fundamental Tasks to slot into the Service Management department quickly and efficiently as required. These Fundamental Tasks could be ignored until they are ready to be implemented, but this could be a negative step because ownership is critical to all ITIL tasks, and to leave ownership identification until the last minute means that the owner will not be able to contribute to the development of the task. This is even more important if the task is to be tightly coupled or integrated with other tasks – the development phase of the task is vital in making sure that the coupling is as tight and as smooth as possible.

7.1.3 Rejected Fundamental Tasks

These are the Fundamental Tasks that will not be included in your Service Management department, though they may reside elsewhere. For example, in an organization where continuity is subjected to a high-risk factor, the Fundamental Task of IT Service Continuity Management may reside in a specialist department with other business-continuity facilities. In some cases the Fundamental Task may be rejected and not exist elsewhere. This is not a finite decision, and you will be able to resurrect these FTs at a later date should the need arise.

7.2 REVIEWING AND GRADING TASKS

The easiest way to rationalize your tasks is to start with a diagram like the one shown in Figure 6.2, ITIL v3 and non-ITIL Fundamental Tasks, and then review and grade each one.

Figure 7.1 shows the diagram from Figure 6.2 with the Fundamental Tasks graded for rationalization. Please note that Figure 7.1 is not intended to show recommended levels of grading or rationalization – it is simply an example, and the grades awarded are for illustration purposes only. However, Figure 7.1 does show how simple it is to illustrate the different ratings diagrammatically.

You may already have an ITIL implementation project or plan in place or in progress. If so, you can use this project to help you to rationalize your Fundamental Tasks. This depends on the nature of the ITIL implementation project – some projects take a very narrow view and only concentrate on one process at a time, which will

Step 5 – Rationalizing the Fundamental Tasks

Figure 7.1 Rationalizing the Fundamental Tasks

Service Strategy	Service Design	Service Operation	Service Transition	Continual Service Improvement
Financial Management	Service Catalogue Management	Event Management	Transition Planning and Support	The 7-Step Improvement Process
Service Portfolio Management	Service Level Management	Incident Management	Change Management	Service Reporting
Demand Management	Capacity Management	Request Fulfilment	Service Asset and Configuration Management	Service Measurement
Business Service Management	Availability Management	Problem Management	Release and Deployment Management	Return on Investment for CSI
SM Governance Management	IT Service Continuity Management	Access Management	Service Validation and Testing	Business Questions for CSI
HR and Education	Information Security Management	Operational Activities and other Lifecycle Phases	Evaluation	
Contract Management	Supplier Management	Service Desk	Knowledge Management	
	Requirements Engineering	Technical Management		
	Data and Information Management	IT Operations Management (Control and Facilities)		
	Business Relationship Management	Applications Management		
	Process Design and Management			

Legend:
- Current Fundamental Tasks
- Planned Fundamental Tasks
- Rejected Fundamental Tasks

not help much with your rationalization. However, you should still consult with the project team to identify which Fundamental Tasks they have on their radar.

Other ITIL implementation projects are more sophisticated and begin by reviewing all the ITIL functions, tasks and processes to identify which will be included in the project. If this is the case, you should work with the project team, as this will save you time and ensure that your department meets the needs of the project. Bear in mind that if you have included non-ITIL Fundamental Tasks, the project team will not be able to contribute anything tangible. However, it is still a good idea to discuss your Fundamental Tasks with them for their ideas and suggestions.

It is unlikely that you will be adopting all the ITIL v3 Fundamental Tasks. If you do, it will be over a long time period, and you may want to alter Figure 7.1 to change the ratings to Current Fundamental Tasks, Phase 1 Fundamental Tasks and Phase 2 Fundamental Tasks, although in some cases you may decide to have three or four phases. This could also apply even if you are only going to adopt a restricted number of ITIL Fundamental Tasks.

7.3 REMOVING THE REJECTED FUNDAMENTAL TASKS

Figure 7.1 contains all the Fundamental Tasks, but if we are going to continue it makes sense to remove the Rejected Fundamental Tasks from the diagram.

In Figure 7.1, 18 Fundamental Tasks have been marked for rejection, leaving the 22 Current and Planned Fundamental Tasks. As you can see in Figure 7.2, the picture now looks clearer. Again, it must be stressed that these have been removed for illustration and discussion purposes only, and this is an example, not a recommendation. To make the picture even clearer, you can rearrange the Fundamental Tasks by their ratings, as shown in Figure 7.3.

Figure 7.2 Current and Planned Fundamental Tasks

Service Strategy	Service Design	Service Operation	Continual Service Improvement
Financial Management	Service Catalogue Management	Event Management	The 7-Step Improvement Process
Service Portfolio Management	Service Level Management	Incident Management	Service Reporting
Demand Management	Capacity Management	Request Fulfilment	Service Measurement
Business Service Management	Availability Management	Problem Management	Return on Investment for CSI
SM Governance Management	Supplier Management	Service Desk	Business Questions for CSI
	Business Relationship Management		
	Process Design and Management		

Current Fundamental Tasks
Planned Fundamental Tasks

Step 5 – Rationalizing the Fundamental Tasks

Figure 7.3 Current and Planned Fundamental Tasks grouped by ratings

Service Strategy	Service Design	Service Operation	Continual Service Improvement
Financial Management	Service Catalogue Management	Event Management	The 7-Step Improvement Process
Business Service Management	Service Level Management	Incident Management	Service Reporting
Service Portfolio Management	Capacity Management	Problem Management	Service Measurement
Demand Management	Availability Management	Service Desk	Return on Investment for CSI
SM Governance Management	Process Design and Management	Request Fulfilment	Business Questions for CSI
	Supplier Management		
	Business Relationship Management		

Legend:
- Current Fundamental Tasks
- Planned Fundamental Tasks

7.4 MEETING THE DEPARTMENTAL PARAMETERS

In Step 2 (Chapter 4), we defined the departmental parameters as a set of rules that would govern the inclusion of the final Fundamental Tasks. Here is a précis of the departmental parameters:

- The ITIL processes, activities and functions should remain as efficient and as intact as possible.
- Other best-practice processes, activities and functions should remain as efficient and as intact as possible.
- The department must meet all governance and legislation requirements.
- The scope of the Fundamental Tasks should encompass more than the ITIL Service Management processes.
- Each Fundamental Task must either be ITIL-conformant or contribute towards meeting the ITIL goals and benefits.

- Fundamental Tasks must connect or integrate logically within an Associated Fundamental Task Pack.
- The Fundamental Tasks within an Associated Fundamental Task Pack should collectively provide a focused level of joint responsibility.
- The Fundamental Tasks in an Associated Fundamental Task Pack should have a common personality.

At this point we have not performed any work on Associated Fundamental Task Packs, so the last three departmental parameters will not apply here. However, the rest of the parameters should be addressed at this point, as some Fundamental Tasks may now be rejected if they do not conform to the departmental parameters. It is better to reject them here than to waste time when creating the Associated Fundamental Task Packs.

7.4.1 Creating a comparison spreadsheet

The concept is simply to compare each Fundamental Task against the first five departmental parameters, to determine how each task conforms, or does not conform, to those parameters. To make this activity easier, we can create a simple spreadsheet, as shown in Figure 7.4.

Figure 7.4 Fundamental Tasks and departmental parameters comparison spreadsheet

Departmental parameters	Current Fundamental Tasks			Planned Fundamental Tasks		
	Task name	Task name	Task name	Task name	Task name	
The ITIL processes, activities and functions should remain as efficient and as intact as possible						
Other best-practice processes, activities and functions should remain as efficient and as intact as possible		N/A				
The department must meet all governance and legislation requirements					N/A	
The scope of the Fundamental Tasks should encompass more than the ITIL Service Management processes		N/A	N/A	N/A	N/A	
Each Fundamental Task must either be ITIL-conformant or contribute towards meeting the ITIL goals and benefits					N/A	

To create and complete the spreadsheet, follow these simple steps:

1. Create a blank spreadsheet template using Figure 7.4 as guide.
2. Enter your departmental parameters in the left-hand column.
3. Enter all your Fundamental Tasks across the top of the columns; for ease of reference, in Figure 7.4 the right-hand columns have been divided into the Current and Planned Fundamental Tasks that we discussed earlier in this chapter.
4. Next, taking one Fundamental Task at a time, compare each one against the departmental parameters.
5. If you fail to meet a departmental parameter, you should document the reason why. If a parameter is not applicable, make a note in the appropriate cell.
6. Document the results of the successful comparisons in the appropriate cells.

These simple steps will take some time to complete. However, they are important to keep the project on course and to deliver the parameters that govern the nature and scope of your Service Management department.

7.5 DOCUMENTING THE RATIONALIZED FUNDAMENTAL TASKS

Once you have completed the spreadsheet, it is important to distribute the results to all interested parties so that they understand if any of the parameters cannot be met. Provide a short written report to accompany the spreadsheet, explaining the key points, along with any observations, ideas and suggestions for reviewing the parameters. Ensure that you get responses from all recipients of the report so that you can take appropriate action.

Step 6 – Creating Associated Fundamental Task Packs

8 Step 6 – Creating Associated Fundamental Task Packs

8.1 DEFINITION OF AN ASSOCIATED FUNDAMENTAL TASK PACK

At this point we have identified and documented our Fundamental Tasks. However, it is very difficult to build a department from numerous disparate tasks. To provide practical building blocks, the Fundamental Tasks that you have identified need to be clustered into logical sets.

For this it is necessary to create Associated Fundamental Task Packs. These are groups of Fundamental Tasks that logically relate to each other, especially in areas such as skill sets, accountability, technology resources and common or similar metrics. Associated Fundamental Task Packs should be self-sufficient, but should contribute fully to a Service Management department. They should have a

Figure 8.1 Example of an Associated Fundamental Task Pack

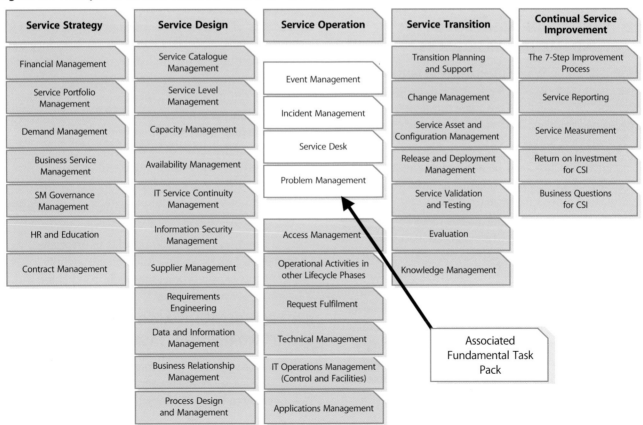

joint level of responsibility so that key metrics such as Key Performance Indicators and Critical Success Factors can be created for them.

To endorse this description, let us look at an example of an Associated Fundamental Task Pack, as shown in Figure 8.1.

In this example, four Fundamental Tasks – Event Management, Incident Management, Service Desk and Problem Management – have been grouped into an Associated Fundamental Task Pack. It is easy to see how these four Fundamental Tasks logically connect with each other, and how the skill sets – accountability, technology resources and common or similar metrics – bridge across the four Fundamental Tasks. This Associated Fundamental Task Pack will be discussed later in this chapter.

8.2 BENEFITS OF ASSOCIATED FUNDAMENTAL TASK PACKS

It is possible to build an ITIL-based Service Management department without using Associated Fundamental Task Packs. However, there are some excellent benefits to be gained from adopting an AFTP approach:

- **Fewer building blocks** A large number of Fundamental Tasks can be reduced to a much smaller number of Associated Fundamental Tasks. This makes designing a department much easier.
- **AFTP discussions** The discussions required to establish Associated Fundamental Task Packs are important as they allow for free discussion and will reduce future confrontation.
- **Technology rationalization** One of the key factors for Associated Fundamental Task Packs is that, whenever possible, the same technology tools are used within a pack. Sometimes, when discussing and creating a pack, additional technology scope can be uncovered, or it may become apparent that a current technology tool could be better utilized.
- **Staff maximization** Staff have different natural skill sets, and although this may seem obvious, it is often overlooked. For example, highly skilled technically focused staff do not often excel in direct communications with a customer. One of the key factors when designing Associated Fundamental Task Packs is to group Fundamental Tasks by skill sets and therefore maximize those natural skills.
- **Increased accountability** Too many traditional departments have simply evolved and their development has not been carefully planned. Often, accountability is spread over different teams or departments, which dilutes responsibilities and accountability. AFTPs make sure that responsibility and accountability are contained within specific boundaries by grouping Fundamental Tasks in logical units.
- **Benefits of smaller organizations** In smaller organizations, Associated Fundamental Tasks may be performed by one person, which makes the grouping of Fundamental Tasks even more important for training and time management.
- **A common personality** When building Associated Fundamental Task Packs, it is important to keep in mind that, as a result of working together, staff teams will develop a common attitude and personality. By creating AFTPs, you can influence that personality and create a positive team attitude, which in turn will lead to better recruitment and training.

This is a summary of the main benefits of Associated Fundamental Task Packs. You will probably identify more benefits as you progress through this chapter.

8.3 ESTABLISHING ASSOCIATED FUNDAMENTAL TASK PACKS

Establishing Associated Fundamental Task Packs is an interesting exercise, as you have to look at each Fundamental Task carefully to examine its relationship with the other

Step 6 – Creating Associated Fundamental Task Packs | 55

Fundamental Tasks. When establishing these relationships, you should involve in the discussions any other interested parties, such as existing teams and managers in the Service Management arena. This will reduce queries or confusion that could occur at a later date when your Service Management department is installed. Throughout this step, keep in mind the departmental parameters and the other key parameters – skill sets, accountability, technology resources and common or similar metrics. Figure 8.2 shows multiple examples of AFTPs.

Figure 8.2 contains the same 40 Fundamental Tasks as in Figure 8.1. Here, however, they have been collated into 11 Associated Fundamental Task Packs. There are three Fundamental Tasks that do not fit readily into any

Figure 8.2 Multiple examples of Associated Fundamental Task Packs

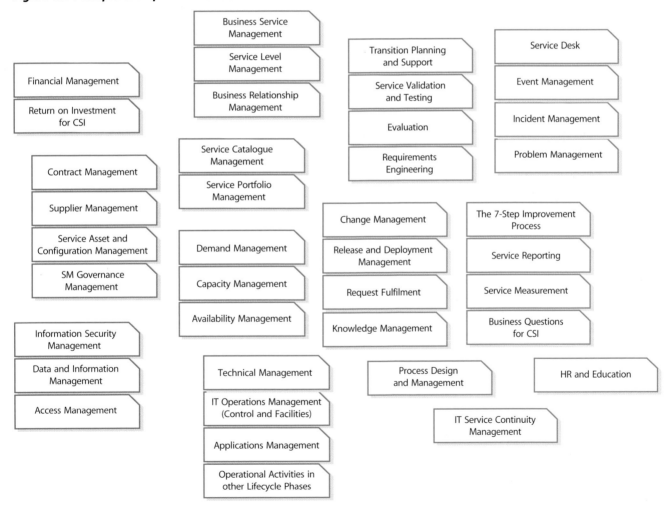

of the AFTPs – these will have to remain as Fundamental Tasks. Please note that these are simply examples, and may not be same as your Associated Fundamental Task Packs. You may also note that they are deliberately misaligned to make the point that at this time they have not been grouped into Departmental Units.

Now let us review these Associated Fundamental Task Packs.

Figure 8.3 Integrity of Service Management

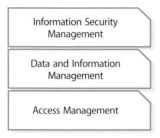

The three Fundamental Tasks in Figure 8.3 have been grouped into a pack because they focus on the integrity of Service Management and its associated services. These Fundamental Tasks require business and security skills and a high degree of accuracy. Staff in this pack will use similar technology, but may need a wide range of tools.

The staff performing these actions may not always be popular with some of the other Service Management staff – as business and IT guardians, they are charged with protecting the integrity of Service Management. The common personality will be studious.

It is easy to see how the Fundamental Tasks in Figure 8.4 work together, as they clearly focus on some of the key legal and contractual FTs. This Associated Fundamental Task Pack can also be regarded as a guardian activity, especially when ensuring that governance requirements are being adhered to.

Figure 8.4 Legal and contractual

The common personality will again be studious, and may require special qualifications or training.

Figure 8.5 Financial

```
Financial Management

Return on Investment
for CSI
```

The financial pack shown in Figure 8.5 is responsible for the key financial elements of IT Service Management. Again, it is a guardian pack, protecting the financial elements. Specialized education and training will be required. The common personality will focus on precision and accuracy.

Figure 8.6 Customer communications

```
Business Service
Management

Service Level
Management

Business Relationship
Management
```

The tasks illustrated in Figure 8.6 concentrate on providing regular communications with the customer, including meeting agreed service levels. The Service Desk will handle the other customer communications. These tasks could be grouped with the next AFTP, but they concentrate on regular daily communications with the customers to solve incidents and handle requests, and as result they have a different personality from the next AFTP, customer information, which is more of a planning function.

Figure 8.7 Customer information

```
Service Catalogue Management
Service Portfolio Management
```

The FTs in Figure 8.7 have been grouped together because they concentrate on building, planning and maintaining vital customer information and knowledge. As a result, they have two common personality traits: staff will typically have to be good communicators with the customers, but will also be expected to keep accurate and detailed records. This AFTP will operate mainly on a tactical level, but occasionally also at both operational and strategic levels.

Figure 8.8 Introduction of new services

Figure 8.8 shows four very important Fundamental Tasks, charged with the successful introduction of new services into Service Management and ensuring that requirements are engineered for new and existing services.

Planning and attention to detail are important parts of the common personality here, and staff will need specialized training and skills. This AFTP will operate mainly at the tactical level, and sometimes at the strategic level.

Figure 8.9 Technology and operational activities

```
Technical Management
IT Operations Management (Control and Facilities)
Applications Management
Operational Activities in other Lifecycle Phases
```

Figure 8.9 illustrates probably the most technical Associated Fundamental Task Pack. It is responsible for technology tools, both new and old; managing new applications throughout their lifecycle; and performing the operational activities required for the successful processing of all applications, systems and services.

This pack requires a high level of technical skills, which are the key ingredients of the common personality. However, many of the skills can be obtained by hands-on training.

Figure 8.10 Demand, capacity and availability

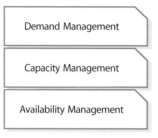

Demand, capacity and availability (see Figure 8.10) are three further Fundamental Tasks that are highly technical and specialized, but are necessary if IT is to meet ever-changing business challenges. Their common personality requires mathematical skills as well as technical knowledge. Typically this AFTP will operate at a tactical level, but will occasionally provide reports to the strategic level.

Figure 8.11 Managing events, incidents and problems

In Figure 8.11 we have the classic components of ITIL Service Management – an Associated Fundamental Task Pack targeted at managing incidents and events and reducing problems. It is also the first line of support for IT customers.

It easy to see how these four Fundamental Tasks fit together. An added bonus is that, to a large degree, they will share technology resources, especially when it comes to recording and managing incidents, events and problems. This AFTP will work mainly at the operational level.

Figure 8.12 Managing change

Figure 8.12 illustrates a critical Associated Fundamental Task Pack, as the successful management of change (and all its associated activities) is essential for a successful Service Management department.

Change Management, Release and Request Fulfilment are obvious candidates to group together. Knowledge Management has Configuration Management as one of its components, and as this relies on change for accuracy, Knowledge Management has been included here.

This AFTP will operate at operational and tactical levels.

The four Fundamental Tasks in the service improvement AFTP (see Figure 8.13) have all been introduced or dramatically updated in the ITIL v3 *Continual Service Improvement* publications. Functionally, these FTs fit together perfectly, and they also have the common objective of improving the service that IT provides to its customers.

Step 6 – Creating Associated Fundamental Task Packs | 59

Figure 8.13 Service improvement

This pack will operate at an operational level, but will occasionally be required to produce reports for strategic-level management.

Figure 8.14 Other Fundamental Tasks

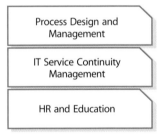

Here in Figure 8.14 we have the final three Fundamental Tasks that do not readily fit into the Associated Fundamental Task Packs. These FTs do have one thing in common, in that their roles and responsibilities may lie outside IT. For example, many enterprises have a specialist group responsible for IT and business continuity; the same could be said for Process Design and HR. The larger the IT Service Management department, the more likely it is that these Fundamental Tasks will be performed by IT Service Management.

8.4 DECIDING ON YOUR FINAL ASSOCIATED FUNDAMENTAL TASK PACKS

A simple tip to use when you are creating your Associated Fundamental Task Packs is to write each Fundamental Task on a card, then lay them face up on a table and 'shuffle' them into Associated Fundamental Task Packs. When you have your first group of AFTPs, use a digital camera to capture your result. You can then repeat this process with input from different people until you have decided on your final set of AFTPs. A graphics package can be used to illustrate the final set of AFTPs.

You may not agree with some of the Associated Fundamental Task Packs or their contents; indeed, you may want to take a completely different approach. Keep an open mind – the AFTPs here are examples to help you, rather than concrete recommendations. One last point to bear in mind is that the number of Fundamental Tasks that you have identified will affect the creation of your Associated Fundamental Task Packs.

8.5 MEETING THE DEPARTMENTAL PARAMETERS

In Step 2 (Chapter 4) we defined the departmental parameters as a set of rules that would govern the inclusion of the final Fundamental Tasks. In Chapter 7 we listed eight parameters (see section 7.4 on meeting the departmental parameters) and have already covered parameters 1–5. The last three parameters are as follows:

- Fundamental Tasks must connect or integrate together logically within an Associated Fundamental Task Pack.
- The FTs within an AFTP should collectively provide a focused level of joint responsibility.
- The FTs in an AFTP should have a common personality.

8.5.1 Creating a comparison spreadsheet

The concept here is simply to compare each Associated Fundamental Task Pack against these last three parameters to determine how each pack conforms, or does not conform, to the parameters. To make this activity easier, create a simple spreadsheet. Figure 8.15 is a modified version of the spreadsheet used for Fundamental Tasks (Figure 7.4).

To create and complete the spreadsheet, follow these simple steps:

1 Create a blank spreadsheet template using Figure 8.15 as guide.
2 Enter your departmental parameters in the left-hand column.
3 Enter all of your Fundamental Task names for an Associated Fundamental Task Pack at the top of each column where you can see 'Fundamental Task #' in Figure 8.15 – one column for each Associated Fundamental Task Pack. For ease of reference, in Figure 8.15 the right-hand columns have been divided into Current and Planned Fundamental Tasks as we discussed in the previous step.
4 Next, taking one AFTP at a time, compare each one against the departmental parameters.
5 If you fail to meet a departmental parameter, you should document the reason why. If a parameter is not applicable, make a note in the appropriate cell.
6 Document the results of the successful comparisons in the appropriate cell.

Figure 8.15 AFTPs and departmental parameters comparison spreadsheet

Parameters	Current AFTPs			Planned AFTPs	
	Fundamental Task #	Fundamental Task #	Fundamental Task #	Fundamental Task #	Fundamental Task #
Fundamental Tasks (FTs) must connect or integrate together logically within an Associated Fundamental Task Pack (AFTP)					
The Fundamental Tasks within an Associated Fundamental Task Pack should collectively provide a focused level of joint responsibility	N/A				
The Fundamental Tasks in an Associated Fundamental Task Pack should have a common personality					

These simple steps will take some time to complete but are important to keep the project on course and to deliver the parameters that govern the nature and scope of your Service Management department.

8.6 DOCUMENTING THE ASSOCIATED FUNDAMENTAL TASK PACKS

Once you have completed the spreadsheet, it is important to distribute the results to all interested parties so that they understand if any of the parameters cannot be met.

Provide a short written report to accompany the spreadsheet, explaining the key points, along with any observations, ideas and suggestions for reviewing the parameters. Ensure that you get responses from all recipients of the report so that you can take appropriate action.

Step 7 – Constructing your Service Management department

9

9 Step 7 – Constructing your Service Management department

9.1 INFLUENCING FACTORS

So far we have discussed many factors that will influence the final design of your Service Management department. There is a danger point in every project where we tend to forge ahead too quickly without considering what we have learned and constructed earlier in the project. We are now at this point, so before continuing we should consider those influencing factors.

9.1.1 Goals and parameters

It is essential to review these here, because your mission statement, goals and parameters will be used by others to assess your final departmental structure. You should refer to the goals and parameters that were used as an example in Figure 4.3.

If the example in Figure 4.3 had been distributed for approval as the mission statement and parameters for a new Service Management department, it is easy to see how this would be used at the end of the project as a measure of success or failure. As you experiment with the final shape and structure of your Service Management department, regularly refer to your mission statement and its associated parameters.

9.1.2 Classic departmental structure

At the beginning of this publication, we discussed the social structure of ancient Egypt and how it stands the test of time when related to a modern departmental structure. It is worth reviewing those lessons here, especially when determining the roles and responsibilities of your department. We will discuss this topic later in this chapter.

9.1.3 Documented materials

Throughout this project, you should have been creating valuable documentation – for example, a description of your Fundamental Tasks. Before progressing further you should re-read these materials to refresh your memory and to ensure that you do not forget any important points.

9.1.4 Taking stock

Of course, there may be many other influencing factors that have emerged so far, and if so you should take them into account. This is the time in the project to take stock before starting the process of creating a departmental template.

9.2 ARRANGING YOUR AFTPS INTO DEPARTMENTAL UNITS

At the completion of the last step, all your Fundamental Tasks should have been grouped into Associated Fundamental Task Packs. It is now necessary to group these tasks one stage further into Departmental Units.

A Departmental Unit is a group of Fundamental Tasks that fit together logically to make an independent component within a department. For example, it could be one of the legs in an organization chart, or could consist of all the Fundamental Tasks under the control of a supervisor or junior manager. This is shown in Figure 9.1.

Figure 9.1 Grouping AFTPs into Departmental Units

Financial Management	Business Service Management	Technical Management	Transition Planning and Support	Service Desk	The 7-Step Improvement Process	HR and Education
Return on Investment for CSI	Service Level Management	IT Operations Management (Control and Facilities)	Service Validation and Testing	Event Management	Service Reporting	Process Design and Management
Contract Management	Business Relationship Management	Applications Management	Evaluation	Incident Management	Service Measurement	
Supplier Management	Service Catalogue Management	Operational Activities in other Lifecycle Phases	Requirements Engineering	Problem Management	Business Questions for CSI	
Service Asset and Configuration Management	Service Portfolio Management	Demand Management		Change Management		
SM Governance Management		Capacity Management		Release and Deployment Management		
Information Security Management		Availability Management		Request Fulfilment		
Data and Information Management				Knowledge Management		
Access Management						
IT Service Continuity Management						

The Associated Fundamental Task Packs used in Figure 9.1 are the same packs that were created in Chapter 8 and illustrated in Figure 8.2 (multiple examples of Associated Fundamental Task Packs). In Figure 9.1 the AFTPs have been grouped into Departmental Units using the same approach and principles that were used in Chapter 8 when the Fundamental Tasks were grouped into Associated Fundamental Task Packs.

The Departmental Units shown in Figure 9.1 relate to each other just as the Fundamental Tasks relate to each other in the Associated Fundamental Task Packs. For example, if you look at the two packs in the second Departmental Unit, column 2 (illustrated in Figure 9.2), you can see how well they fit together. Here we have two AFTPs concerned with service levels and customer relations. The first AFTP is concerned with communicating with the customers, while the second AFTP is more of an administration function. Even though they are both involved with service, they require different common personalities. They combine perfectly to make a complete Departmental Unit, providing a focused level of service to IT Service Management customers. We can see this trend reflected in the other Departmental Units.

Figure 9.2 A complete Departmental Unit

So, remember to use the lessons and principles from Chapter 8 concerning Associated Fundamental Task Packs to create your Departmental Units.

9.3 NAMING DEPARTMENTAL UNITS

We need to give names to our Departmental Units. Ideally, these names need to be short and descriptive. Some examples are shown in Figure 9.3.

The names used here are just for descriptive purposes – you could, of course, select your own names that are more meaningful to the Departmental Units that you have created. The rationale for these names is discussed below, to demonstrate the logic and approach required to allocate simple yet descriptive titles.

9.3.1 Integrity Management

The *Oxford Dictionary of English* describes integrity as 'the quality of being honest and morally upright. The state of being whole or unified and/or the soundness of construction'. This is a great description for this Departmental Unit because it is responsible for the integrity of IT service management and beyond.

9.3.2 Customer Management

This is a good name as this Departmental Unit is responsible for the management of all operational contact with IT customers, except for the communication required to support the daily operations activities, such as Service Desk, and Change Management. This title does suggest that ITSM is managing customers rather than working in unison with them, so you may prefer a title such as 'Customer Liaison'.

9.3.3 Operations Management

This Departmental Unit is responsible for the daily operation (plus the processes and tasks required to maintain the successful operation of production systems and services) of IT systems, services and applications. Hence 'Operations Management' is an apt title.

Figure 9.3 Naming the Departmental Units

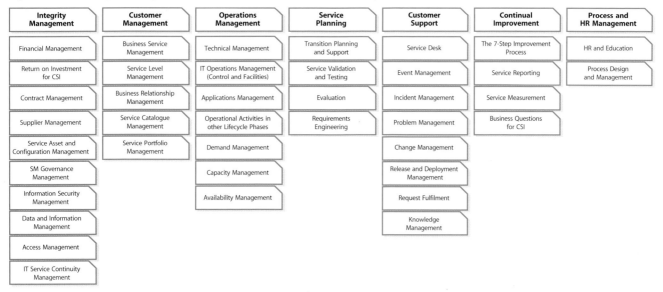

9.3.4 Service Planning

It was hard to find a descriptive name for this Departmental Unit because it does not have such clear objectives as some of the others. However, as this Departmental Unit is chiefly concerned with bringing new services into IT, Service Planning seemed to be the most appropriate name.

9.3.5 Customer Support

Naming this Departmental Unit was quite simple, as it is the provider of daily support for the IT business community. It also contains many of the processes that are part of Service Support in ITIL version 2.

9.3.6 Continual Improvement

This was another easy name to create, because it perfectly describes the Fundamental Tasks in this unit, especially since most of the processes described in the ITIL version 3 publication *Continual Service Improvement* are contained in this Departmental Unit.

9.3.7 Process and HR Management

This was another easy name to identify as it lists the two processes that would not fit comfortably in any of the other Departmental Units.

Figure 9.4 Final department structure

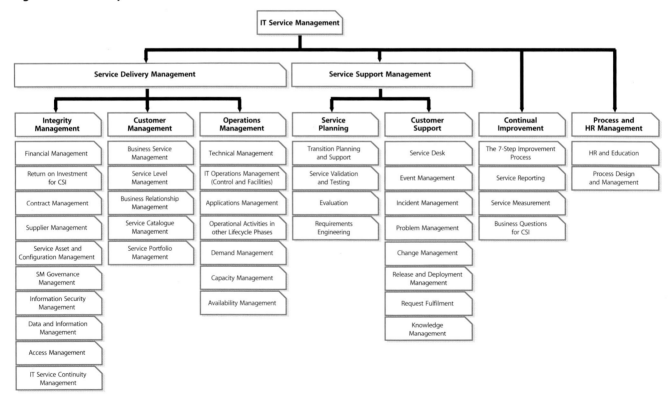

9.4 FINALIZING THE CONSTRUCTION

Now we must group the Departmental Units under a management layer. It is impossible in this publication to anticipate the management layers that you will need, as this depends on your company's management structures, the potential size of your Service Management department and the Departmental Units that you have created. Figure 9.4 provides an example for illustrative purposes only.

In Figure 9.4, two tiers of management have been added to the Departmental Units shown in Figure 9.3. The upper level, IT Service Management, is the most senior, responsible for the daily management of IT service, while the lower level is the front-line management level, which is often called the supervisory level.

There is a key difference between these two tiers. The upper level concentrates on managing the department and is responsible for activities such as building budgets, allocating headcount, handling appraisals and future departmental planning. The lower level is responsible for ensuring that the scheduled daily tasks are completed to a predetermined standard, that staff are motivated, daily targets are met, and that management are fully informed if any problems or anomalies occur. It is important to illustrate these as separate levels when creating a departmental structure or departmental template.

The departmental structure shown in Figure 9.4 shows one example of how your final Service Management department could look, but it is probable that your department may look very different. This would be due to the nature of your business and the Fundamental Tasks that you have rejected. Let us have a look at a different departmental template to keep an open mind (see Figure 9.5).

As you can see, this is an entirely different approach; it has fewer columns, but the same number of Fundamental Tasks. Figure 9.4 had a focus on Service Delivery and Service Support, which very much reflects ITIL version 2, even though all of the Fundamental Tasks are from ITIL version 3 (except, of course, the non-ITIL Fundamental Tasks). Figure 9.5 has a different focus:

- **Service Integrity** is essentially the same, charged with protecting the integrity of both Service Management and the customers. However, there is one subtle difference, as HR and Education have been added here. This is because maintaining Service Integrity also depends on employing the correct personnel.
- **Service Planning** contains all of the elements required to maintain the current and future IT Service Management commitments. It includes Change Management because changes require planning and the 7-Step Improvement Process because this, too, often requires planning. Note also that Process Design and Management have been included here; this is so that the responsibility for planning processes is centralized in one place.
- **Service Operations** – the focus here is on those daily and scheduled activities that have to be performed to ensure that all services are functioning to agreed service levels. Availability and Capacity Management have been included here as they are vital to meet SLAs, but could quite easily have been included in Service Planning.
- Here **Service Support** covers both Customer Management, as seen in Figure 9.4, and most of Customer Support, also from Figure 9.4. The idea is to concentrate all customer contact and relations in one place, thus focusing responsibilities and accountabilities.

If you gave two top chefs the same set of ingredients and asked them to cook a meal of their choice, you would get two great meals, but it is highly unlikely that you would get the same meals. The same applies here: the same ingredients – Fundamental Tasks – but a different outcome. You will find more departmental templates in the appendices.

Figure 9.5 Alternative departmental template

9.5 DEPARTMENTAL CHARACTERISTICS

Now that we have created a departmental template it is time to bring the ancient Egyptians back. In the first chapter of this publication we discussed the social structure of the ancient Egyptians and learned how this structure could apply to a modern IT Service Management department. In particular we identified eight questions that you should ask of each of the Fundamental Tasks in your final department structure. The first three questions apply to the management layer; the rest apply to the other layers in the structure. Figure 9.6 shows the questions as they relate to the ancient and modern structures.

Step 7 – Constructing your Service Management department | 71

Figure 9.6 Departmental characteristics: the eight key questions

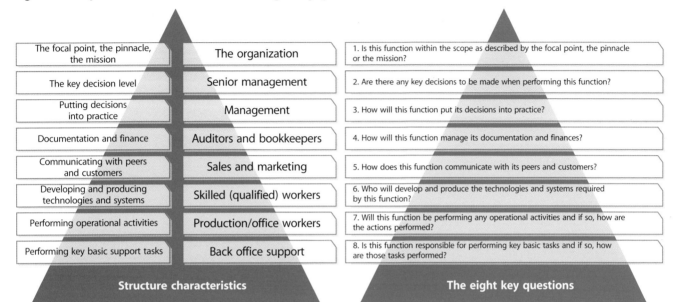

Look at each of your Fundamental Tasks to identify which questions apply to them. For each Fundamental Task, find the question that has the most significance to that task so that you can plot its place in the hierarchy.

In Figure 9.7 we have used the same template that we used in Figure 9.5, but have grouped the Fundamental Tasks to reflect the ancient Egypt social structure after posing the eight questions for each task. This involves a series of simple and logical steps:

1. Create a departmental template following the instructions earlier in this publication.
2. Review the ancient and modern structures.
3. Decide how many levels you are going to include to determine the character of your department, Figure 9.6 shows the original eight levels.
4. Create a question, or questions, that can be used to identify which is the prime characteristic for a Fundamental Task. Figure 9.6 shows some example questions as they relate to each level.
5. Pose each of the questions against each of the Fundamental Tasks and document the results.
6. Once you have posed the question, or questions, for each Fundamental Task, you can then allocate them a characteristic with which they are most compatible.
7. You can now group your Fundamental Tasks by characteristic within your departmental template, and the result is Figure 9.7.

Some Fundamental Tasks may be so flexible that they are compatible with more than one characteristic. For example, in Figure 9.7 you will see that Change Management is included at both the Scribe and the Artisan levels, because there is such a huge difference between managing a change and performing the actions to implement a change. However, this should be seen as an exception. What we are trying to do is build a healthy department that functions successfully on all levels. If many Fundamental Tasks are duplicated, you will dilute the result, so try to stick to one level per Fundamental Task.

Figure 9.7 represents a healthy department, with clearly identified Fundamental Tasks at each level within the structure. Each of the levels shown in earlier chapters, and again in Figure 9.6, is important to the nature and personality of a department. Without these characteristics a department could be a difficult place in which to work. Table 9.1 lists some of the implications of not having good departmental characteristics.

Figure 9.7 Departmental characteristics

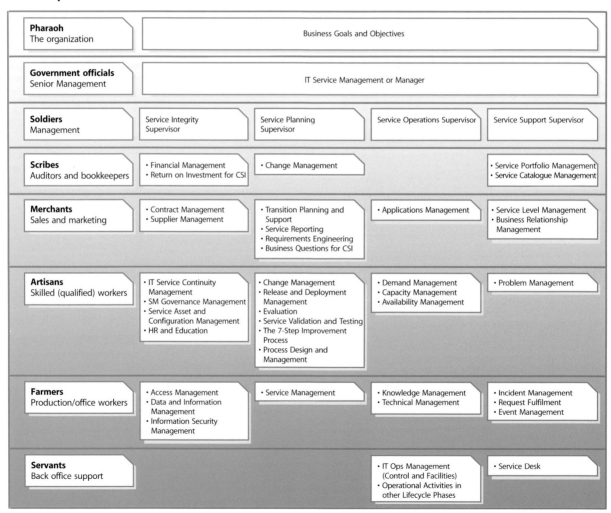

Table 9.1 Departmental structural levels and their importance

Structural level	Implication of not having clearly defined structural levels
The focal point, the pinnacle, the mission	Without a focal point, a pinnacle or a mission statement, it is very difficult to create Critical Success Factors and Key Performance Indicators that relate to the business. Without these, staff can be set internal targets but will not be able to relate their role to the business targets, and as a result will see themselves as an independent small unit, isolated within the organization.
The key decision level	One of the keys to a successful department is the ability to make and communicate decisions. Without this, anarchy reigns: units will decide on their own rules and make isolated decisions that benefit only themselves.
Putting decisions into practice	Most people have seen a good practice at work fail because some staff ignore the practice or oppose it for their own self-serving reasons. This confuses peer departments who believe that the decisions have been put into practice and are being obeyed. A department that does not make sensible decisions and does not have the strength to ensure that those decisions are followed is often a confrontational and unpleasant place in which to work.
Documentation and finance	A department that cannot justify or manage its budget is a stressful place to work. Equally, a department without documentation leads to confusion and contradictory working practices.
Communicating with peers and customers	Communication is vital to Service Management. A Service Management department that cannot communicate with its customers and peers on many levels will not last long.
Developing and producing technologies and systems	Service Management cannot survive without the correct supporting technology – for example, how long would a Service Desk survive if every incident had to be logged manually?
Performing operational activities	The key difference between this level and the following level, Performing key basic support tasks, is the ability to take actions and to control activities. For example, in Figure 9.7 some of the Fundamental Tasks included at this level are Incident Management, Request Fulfilment and Event Management, which require analysis and problem-solving skills. If these tasks are not performed, Service Management simply becomes a conduit for other IT departments.
Performing key basic support tasks	The final level is important because it underpins all the other levels. For example, the basic role of a Service Desk is to collate and document incidents: if this is not performed correctly, Incident and Problem Management cannot function effectively, whether they are performed by the Service Desk or another Associated Fundamental Task Pack.

As you can see, the implications of not having clear departmental characteristics are dramatic. Departmental characteristics determine how Service Management is rated, so it makes sense to put the effort in now to create a successful department.

Ideally, you should have at least one Fundamental Task at each structural level. This may not always be possible – for example if your department does not have many Fundamental Tasks – but make sure that you have a valid reason for not including any Fundamental Tasks at a certain level. Allocating your Fundamental Tasks to the various department levels is a very subjective undertaking – Figure 9.7 is an illustration only, and may not reflect your own departmental characteristics.

Step 8 – Organizational plans and charts

10 Step 8 – Organizational plans and charts

Figure 10.1 Alternative departmental template plan with added AFTPs

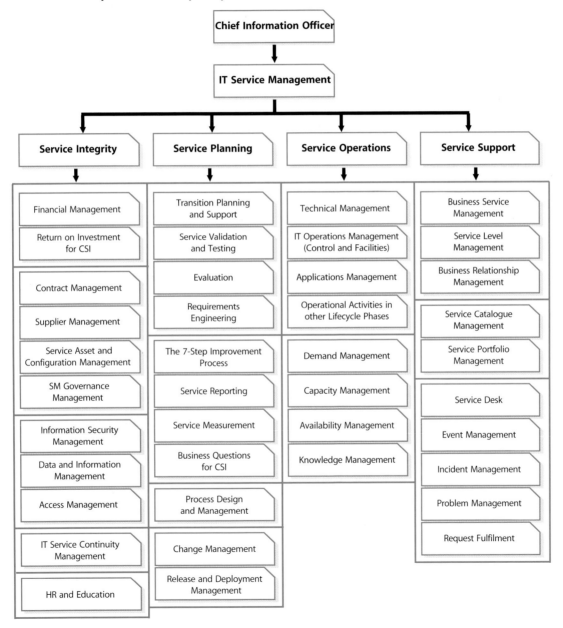

You now need to turn your attention to your organization plan and organization chart. These are very subjective, and most organizations have different rules governing their organizational charts. Therefore, here we concentrate on the construction of organization charts rather than on specific styles of chart.

10.1 ORGANIZATIONAL PLANS

Organizational plans are a transitional step to help you to create organizational charts. Departmental templates and Associated Fundamental Task Packs are great aids in the construction of organization charts and plans. Figure 10.1 shows the template used in Figure 9.5, Alternative departmental template, but with the addition of the Associated Fundamental Task Packs and the senior management layer.

As you can see, there is a clear resemblance between this template and an organization chart; in fact, if your organization does not have any firm rules concerning organization charts, you could probably use this format.

The following illustrations (Figures 10.2 to 10.6) show how easy it can be to convert the template in Figure 10.1 into an organization plan.

It is impossible to show the complete organization plan here, so for convenience it has been broken into components. Figure 10.2 shows the management level, which is straightforward and reflects the eight layers of the classical departmental characteristics. It already resembles an organizational chart. The next levels are indicated by the numbers 1 to 4 in Figure 10.2, and are shown in further detail in Figures 10.3 to 10.6.

Figure 10.2 Organization plan at management level

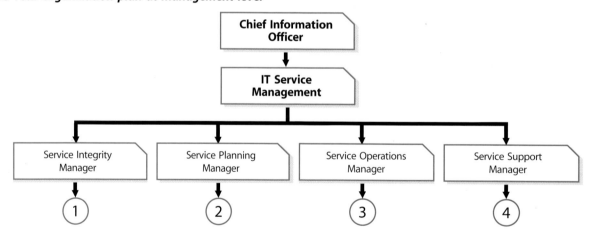

Figure 10.3 Organizational plan for Service Integrity

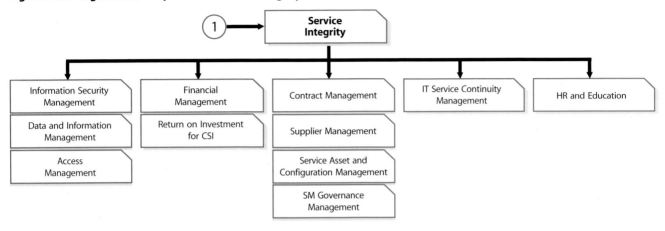

Figure 10.4 Organizational plan for Service Planning

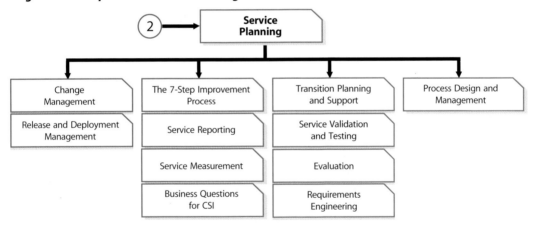

Figure 10.5 Organizational plan for Service Operations

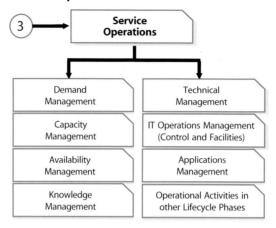

Figure 10.6 Organizational plan for Service Support

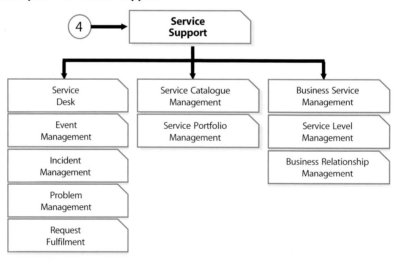

As you have probably noticed, Figures 10.3 to 10.6 show the Associated Fundamental Task Packs listed horizontally rather than vertically. If you want your organizational plan to also reflect status, then you may need to change the order of the Fundamental Tasks.

It is also important to remember that the FTs are not necessarily jobs, because in a smaller organization one person may perform several FTs in a day. We can use these charts to produce our organization charts.

10.2 ORGANIZATIONAL CHARTS

Organizational charts do not contain lists of Fundamental Tasks like organization plans, but contain the job titles responsible for performing the Fundamental Tasks. This is one of the reasons why the Associated Fundamental Task Packs are so important, because you can get the situation where an organization chart has, for example, Service Desk Analyst as a job title, but it does not tell you that the Service Desk Analyst is also responsible for Event Management, Incident Management, Problem Management and Request Fulfilment as Figure 10.7 shows.

Figure 10.7 Migrating from an organizational plan to an organizational chart

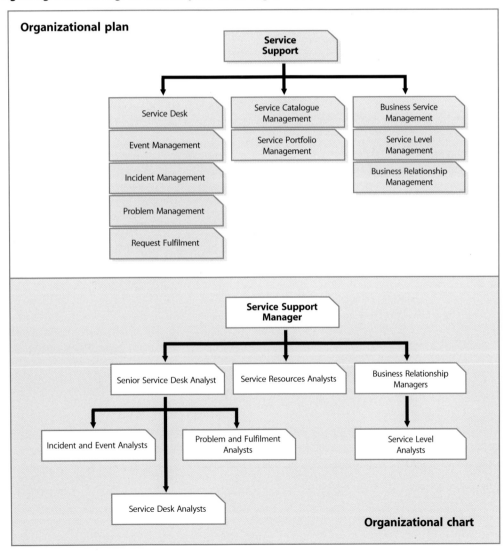

Figure 10.7 shows how easy it is to migrate from an organizational plan to an organizational chart. The top half of the graphic is from Figure 10.6 and shows the organizational plan, while the bottom half of the graphic is that plan translated into an organizational chart. The bottom half follows a classic organizational chart format, with each column showing the hierarchy of the jobs and each row showing the comparative status of those jobs. So we can see that the Senior Service Desk Analyst, the Service Resources Analysts and the Business Relationship Managers all have the same status, as do the Incident and Event Analysts, the Problem and Fulfilment Analysts and the Service Level Analysts, whereas the Service Desk Analysts have the lowest status in this chart.

Having both organizational plans and charts helps to keep clear the relationships between job titles and the tasks performed by those jobs. Migrating from organizational plans to organizational charts should be straightforward. However, if your organization uses a template for organization charts that reflects the levels and status of roles, then you should make sure that you follow your organizational standards.

10.3 SUMMARY

Organization plans are extremely useful when creating organizational charts. However, they are not required by most organizations, which means that you may be tempted to bypass them. In the case of small departments this may not be a problem, but for larger departments organization plans are important in understanding the nature and shape of your department.

Step 9 – Resourcing your Service Management department

11

11 Step 9 – Resourcing your Service Management department

Once you have built your Service Management department, the final stage is to provide the resources required to make your department fully functional by completing activities such as job descriptions, processes, work instructions and technology. In some cases these may already be in place, but you still need to review them as part of resourcing your department.

All of the previous steps have been individual building blocks, but this one is different because once you have created your organizational plans and charts, this step will need to be repeated for each Associated Fundamental Task Pack or, in some cases, for individual Fundamental Tasks.

11.1 JOB DESCRIPTIONS

Now that you have created your organizational charts, you should be in a position to create your job descriptions. Very often job descriptions fall between two stools – describing the job and explaining the importance and significance of the job. You can have a job description that accurately describes the tasks of a job but does not explain the importance of those tasks, and the result is an under-graded job. Of course, you can also get the opposite effect by overstating the importance of a job, the result of which can be an over-graded job. Neither result is desirable, as sooner or later there will be uneasiness amongst the staff.

Job descriptions are very subjective and usually have to conform to a corporate standard in both content and structure. Therefore, it is difficult to provide much advice here, except some tips and hints.

- **Importance interfaces** Some roles involve communicating with staff at every level in the organization. For example, a call to the Service Desk from the newest junior employee in an organization can be followed by a call from the Chief Information Officer. Make sure that you clearly state the level of all interfaces that the job is likely to involve.
- **Customer interfaces** If any of the jobs in Service Management involve contact with external customers, it is extremely important that these relationships are clearly described, especially the frequency and level of those contacts and the reasons for them.
- **Vendor communications** Many of the jobs within Service Management will require communications with vendors, such as technology vendors, outsourcers and other suppliers. Again it is important to describe these clearly, especially the frequency and level of the communications and the reasons for them. If the job involves recommending investment in the purchase or leasing of technologies, it is very important to explain this role.
- **Implications to customers and business** These implications are most concerned with the potential impact of mistakes and errors on customers or the business. For example, a Service Desk Analyst may allocate the wrong priority to an incident and as a result lose valuable business time through reduced IT availability. Make sure that you mention potential impacts because they are often the true measure of a job.
- **Secrecy and confidentiality** Some of the roles in Service Management are involved with tasks such as access management, contracts, data management and

governance, all of which can have strict security controls. Always make sure that security and governance implications are included in any Service Management job descriptions.

- **Accuracy** Some jobs with seemingly simple, repetitive functions require very high levels of accuracy. The Service Desk is a good case: although there are many simple, repetitive actions, these must be performed quickly and with great accuracy, which requires high levels of concentration and analytical skills. Make sure that you include the performance and accuracy levels for those repetitive tasks to ensure that their true nature is fully understood.
- **Pressure and stress** Every job in Service Management is subjected to stress, though the stress elements may be very different. For example, the Service Desk never gets a rest from the continual flow of incidents, while a Security Manager is constantly on the lookout for security breaches. You should not overemphasize stress and pressure except where they are obviously part of the job, and when they are part of the job you should state the levels of stress very clearly.
- **Ensure contractual compliance** Service Management interface with many contracts during the average working day, ranging from break-and-fix engineering service to software licence compliance. Many of these contracts involve high investment levels and serious implications for breach of contract on both sides. Therefore, if a job in Service Management comes into close contact with the creation or employment of a contract, this should be stated in the job description.

There are many more considerations that could be added to the list – for example, time management and analytical analysis. Make full use of your organizational plans and the ITIL publications when creating your job descriptions.

11.2 PROCESSES AND WORK INSTRUCTIONS

Processes and work instructions are not the same – processes tell you when and how quickly to perform a task, whereas work instructions tell you what to do and how well to perform that task. Here is an example for escalating an incident.

1 **Process** The next step in the process is to escalate the incident. Each step in a process points to the next step to be performed. The time to get from one step to another is measured as a performance metric and is the mean time between steps (MTBS).

2 **Process** It has to be escalated within two minutes. An amount of time is usually allocated to each step in a process. Again this is a performance metric, and is the mean time to action a step (MTAS). When one part of a process is complete, the sum of all MTBS and MTAS is the time that it took to complete the process: mean time to process (MTTP).

3 **Work instruction** I have to escalate to Network Administration. This work instruction should tell me exactly what actions and references I need to complete this step. In this case, it should tell me how I decide who to allocate the incident to, and how I send the incident to them.

4 **Work instruction** I have to escalate to the correct person first time 99% of the time, which is a quality metric to ensure that the tasks are performed to a given standard.

So in theory there are four components to each step of a process, ensuring high performance to a designated level of quality. It is the merging of processes and work instructions that guarantees success. When building your department, you must ensure that all processes and work instructions are complete. Many of the Fundamental Tasks that you have included in your department will include existing versions of those processes and work

Figure 11.1 Process metrics

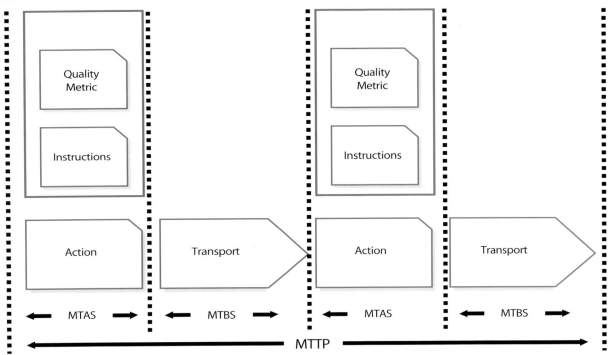

instructions. Make sure that you check these inherited facilities thoroughly against the v3 process descriptions, to ensure that they will fit neatly into your new department.

Do not make the mistake of ignoring work instructions in favour of processes. It is just as important, if not more important, to know what to do as when to do it. Many processes are simple and repetitive, whereas work instructions can be complex. For example, allocating a priority and escalating an incident are two simple steps in a process but can be quite complex work instructions, especially if business rules are to apply along with IT instructions. One of the main roles for Service Management software is to automate these processes and follow the work instructions, so the better you have built the work instructions, the more likely it is that you will successfully select and implement the correct software.

If you do not have documented processes and work instructions, more training will be required, and new staff will take longer to become effective. Make sure that you create your processes and work instructions as you bring your Fundamental Tasks into your departments.

11.3 SERVICE MANAGEMENT TECHNOLOGY

Service Management technology depends on which Fundamental Tasks you have included in your department and varies dramatically in complexity. For example, you may need various tools to calculate the capacity of different platforms, but only one tool for Incident Management. Here are a few hints and tips to help you to select your technology.

11.3.1 ITIL compatibility

If you are using ITIL as your best practice, it makes sense to try to use software that is ITIL-conformant with the version of ITIL that you are embracing. Ensure that potential vendors demonstrate their ITIL compatibility, and make sure that you have some examples from your own processes for them to prove that compatibility.

11.3.2 Suite approach

When looking for technology solutions to apply to Service Management, you can either select the best individual solutions for each Fundamental Task or look for a suite covering a number of FTs. Remember a few years ago when we searched for the very best word processor, the very best calendar tool, the very best spreadsheet and the very best graphics package – each one top of the range but often incompatible with each other. Now we just look for the best packaged solution, e.g. Microsoft Office. The same applies for Service Management software: in the ideal world, we would be able to find technology that would support a complete Associated Fundamental Task Pack – for example, the Service Desk, Incident Management, Problem Management and Event Management. This AFTP is better as a suite. You should look for suite solutions whenever possible.

11.3.3 Good processes and work instructions

We have already mentioned the need for well-documented processes and work instructions and how they can help with the selection of software. You should use these to create some scenarios to test any potential technology solutions. If you use the same scenarios for all potential technology, you will get a consistent set of results to compare. Do not allow potential vendors to select their own scenarios, because it is almost certain that these have been built to showcase their products. Remember, the better the process and work instructions, the more likely it is you will select the correct technology and maximize the usage of that technology.

11.3.4 Scalability

Scalability may not apply to every organization, but it is still an important point to consider. The key question is: will there be any potential expansion for Service Management and, if so, what will be the scale of the growth? Obviously you will be looking for a solution that can meet your anticipated capacity, but if this is to be achieved through growth over a given period, you may want to select a product that allows you to pay only for the technology that you need at any given time. For example, you may start with 10 people on your service and expand that to 50 over a two-year period, in which case you would only want to pay for the licences as you need them.

11.3.5 Compatibility

Be very aware of the difference between 'yes, it will work on that platform' and 'we can make it work on that platform, no problem'. Incompatibility between different technologies is time-consuming, expensive and a hindrance to future updates. If the proposed technology is not proven to be compatible with your existing technologies, then you should think twice before purchasing.

11.3.6 Usability

This is an important component, but not easy to quantify. Opinions can differ widely, depending on the look and feel of a technology solution. For example, there are those people who like a graphical approach, and those who prefer a high screen-content level. Usability can be very subjective, but is often related to knowledge and usage levels. For example, a Service Desk Analyst may prefer a detailed screen explaining all the relevant data when a failure occurs, whereas a customer may require a simple graphic indicating which services have failed.

Identify all the potential users of proposed technologies to establish the levels of usability that you will require, but do not get enticed into spending huge amounts of time trying to please everybody. If you have discord, then you must make sure that the usability meets the needs of the prime users of the technology.

11.3.7 Functionality (e.g. updating tables)

With many Service Management technologies there will be a need regularly to update screen layouts, tables, etc. For example, a new application could mean that the change parameters need to be updated. Ideally, the team using a product should be able to update parameters and tables themselves to reduce changes and to maximize their resources. Even if you have a specialized unit to perform this action, make sure that managing the functionality of a product is not too time-consuming.

11.3.8 Maintenance/upgrades

Checking the frequency and costs of maintenance, support and upgrades is a basic requirement for the purchasing of any technologies. Make sure that you give this serious consideration when purchasing a product.

11.3.9 Vendor partnerships

Vendors are no longer the enemy to be treated with aggression and disdain. They have considerable knowledge and experience in Service Management, and are prepared to share this with you to help you maximize the potential products, as long as you treat them as partners rather than as the opposition. Utilize their experience and you will save time and money.

11.3.10 Needs analysis

It is important that you spend time creating a needs analysis report before purchasing any technology solutions. You must know exactly what you need and how it should function. If you do not do this before viewing products, you can get seduced away from your requirements by fancy features that you do not need.

A needs analysis report should not be secret. Make sure that your potential vendors see and understand the report: this will save future confrontations due to 'misunderstandings'. If you do not know how to create a needs analysis, ask for help from other people in your IT department. Use your needs analysis report to select potential vendors and to test the functions and features of their products. You can use all of the tips and hints listed here to help you to create your needs analysis.

11.3.11 Selecting the technology

Like many other departments, Service Management is technology-dependent, but what makes it unique is the amount of human interfacing skills required by Service Management. For example a great Service Desk product will reduce the amount of time needed to enter information, and as a result will allow a Service Desk Analyst more time to concentrate on the incident and the customer. Take your time and make sure that you select the correct technology because you only get one chance – get it wrong and you will have to live with your mistake.

11.4 SUMMARY

Organization plans and charts are invaluable tools when resourcing your Service Management department – make full use of them. There are other components that you will have to consider – skills charts, training, education, staffing levels and budgets are some of the more obvious components – but as these are so subjective, it is impossible to discuss them in any detail here.

Implementing your Service Management department

12

12 Implementing your Service Management department

12.1 PREPARING A PHASED PLAN

It is unlikely that you will want to attempt to implement your complete Service Management department in one go. You will probably prefer to phase the implementation in stages. The first step is to prepare a phased approach map, as shown in Figure 12.1.

The layout in Figure 12.1 has been used already in some of the earlier chapters to illustrate how Fundamental Tasks and Associated Fundamental Task Packs are created. This time we will use it to explain how a phased approach can be taken to implement a Service Management department.

Figure 12.1 Phased approach map

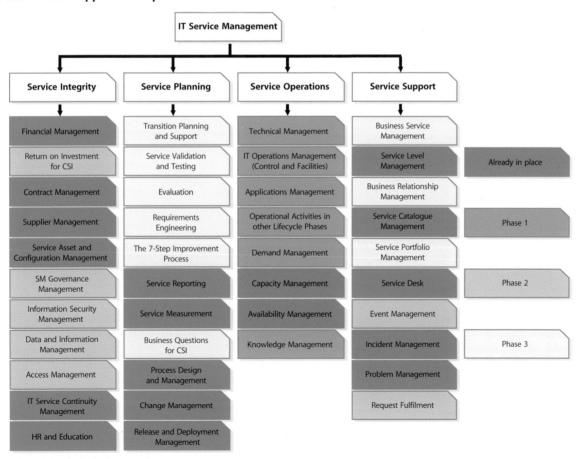

1 First of all take your departmental plan.
2 Identify those Fundamental Tasks that are already in place.
3 Arrange the rest of the Fundamental Tasks into logical groups. It is up to you how you arrange the FTs into phases. For example, the map in Figure 12.1 has three phases. Phase 1 is primarily targeted at the operational Fundamental Tasks; Phase 2 is aimed mainly at integrity; while Phase 3 concerns continual improvement and customer relations. This is just a suggestion, but logical groups make most sense rather than an across-the-board attack.

For those Fundamental Tasks that you identified as already being in place, you should perform gap analysis, comparing each of them against ITIL version 3 to identify the shortfall between your processes and the v3 process specifications. If you are not following ITIL, you will have to create a standard against which to measure each Fundamental Task. It may be that, for various reasons, you are going to tailor the ITIL v3 definition to meet your specific requirements. If this is the case, you should create this definition and then perform gap analysis. Once you have completed your gap analysis, you should perform any actions required to eliminate any gaps before proceeding.

Figure 12.2 ITIL v2 to v3 transitioning phased approach map

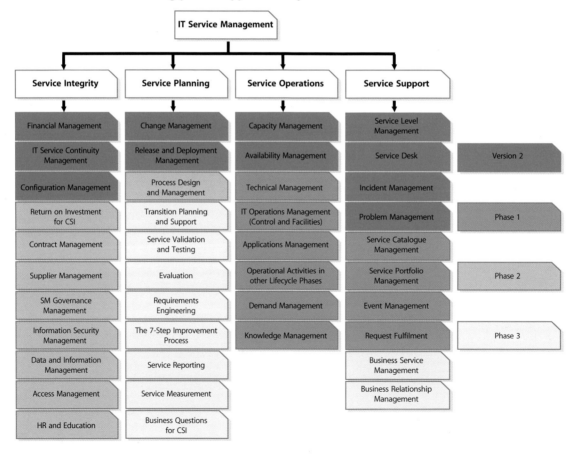

You may want to take a slightly different approach if you already have v2 successfully implemented and want to transition to v3. In this case you should consider altering the contents of your phased approach map to isolate the v2 components that you have already implemented.

Figure 12.2 is essentially the same as Figure 12.1, except that the v2 components have been moved to the top of their respective legs, while the v3 components have been grouped by their implementation phases. Figure 12.2 is easier to follow, but does not reflect the Associated Fundamental Task Packs.

You will need to prepare a plan or a project to implement your Service Management department. You can use the structure of this publication as your reference source to create your plan.

Steps 1–8 are all individual steps, but Step 9 will need to be repeated for each Fundamental Task until full implementation is completed. Each of these steps should be regarded as Gateways, which means that you should document and obtain approval for each one before proceeding to the next step.

Table 12.1 Implementation plan

Step	Task	Activity
1		Preparing the basics
	1	Repetitive step groups
	2	Selecting a project team
	3	Collating current materials
	4	Other ITIL projects
2		Defining departmental parameters
	1	Creating a mission statement
	2	Creating departmental parameters
3		Primary ITIL Fundamental Tasks
	1	Identifying the ITIL Fundamental Tasks
	2	Documenting the ITIL Fundamental Tasks
4		Identifying non-ITIL Fundamental Tasks
	1	Preparing to locate non-ITIL Fundamental Tasks
	2	Identifying the non-ITIL Fundamental Tasks
	3	Documenting non-ITIL Fundamental Tasks

Step	Task	Activity
5		**Rationalizing the Fundamental Tasks**
	1	Rationalizing the Fundamental Tasks
	2	Removing the Rejected Fundamental Tasks
	3	Meeting the departmental parameters
	4	Documenting the rationalized Fundamental Tasks
6		**Creating Associated Fundamental Task Packs**
	1	Benefits of Associated Fundamental Task Packs
	2	Establishing Associated Fundamental Task Packs
	3	Meeting the departmental parameters
	4	Documenting the Associated Fundamental Task Packs
7		**Constructing your department template**
	1	Influence factors
	2	Arranging your AFTPs into Departmental Units
	3	Naming Departmental Units
	4	Finalizing construction
	5	Departmental characteristics
8		**Organizational plans and charts**
	1	Organizational plans
	2	Organizational charts
9		**Resourcing your Service Management department – repeat for each FT**
	1	Job descriptions
	2	Processes and work instructions
	3	Service Management technology

Example of an ITIL version 2 departmental template

Appendix A: Example of an ITIL version 2 departmental template

Most organizations only employed two of the ITIL v2 seven core publications, *Service Support* and *Service Delivery*, and as a result had far fewer processes and functions to implement. This meant that the department templates were a lot simpler, as the following example illustrates.

All of the 10 processes and one function from the ITIL v2 *Service Support* and *Service Delivery* publications are included in Figure A.1. The management layer reflects the publications, except that a third leg has been added for technical support. This is a classic approach, and for existing ITIL v2 organizations could be used as a starting point from which to develop a v3 departmental template.

Figure A.1 Example of an ITIL version 2 departmental template

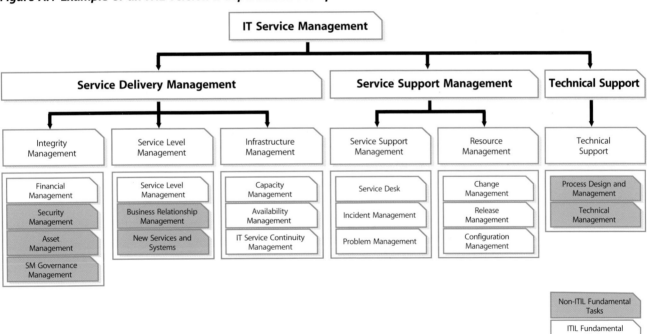

Example of an ITIL version 3 departmental template

B

Appendix B: Example of an ITIL version 3 departmental template

As you would expect, a departmental template for ITIL v3 is more comprehensive than a departmental template for ITIL v2, which only includes service support and service delivery.

This example, shown in Figure B.1, is based around the five ITIL v3 publications, with each publication represented as a separate leg. This approach looks ideal because it mirrors the publications, but it makes it very difficult to allocate responsibilities for some of the disciplines, as Figure B.2 illustrates.

Figure B.1 Example of an ITIL version 3 departmental template

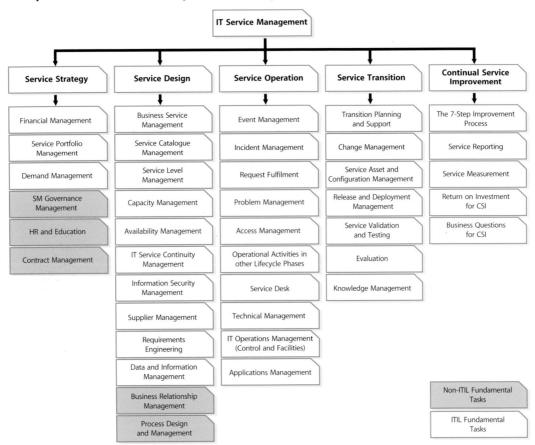

Figure B.2 is a diluted version of Figure B.1, where all of the Fundamental Tasks have been removed, except for those that relate directly to Service Management. The key question here is who takes the overall responsibility for service? You can just imagine some of the meetings with five Departmental Units all sharing some responsibilities.

In the examples used in this publication, the Fundamental Tasks have been grouped into Associated Fundamental Task Packs by responsibility to ensure that responsibilities are clear at all times.

Figure B.2 Dissipated Service Management disciplines

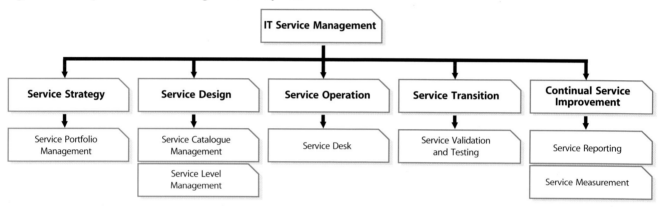

Index

Index

Note: Page numbers that refer only to figures and tables are in italics.

Access Management 56
accountability 54
account management 10
accuracy 86
activity, definition 29
advisers 20
AFTPs 16, 25, 49, 80, 81, 88, *96*, 104
    creating 53–61
    definition 23–4
    into Departmental Units 65–6
analysis, gap 94
ancient Egypt, social structure 4–5, 6–7, 8, 71–2
approval 95
artisans 5, 7, *72*
Associated Fundamental Task Packs *see* AFTPs
associations, industry 37
attitude, team 54
auditors 7, *72*
Availability Management 58, 69

back office support 7, 8
barter 7
benefits 25, 48
bookkeepers 7
budgeting 10
building blocks 54
Business Relationship Management 40, *56*, 57
Business Service Management 39, *56*, 57

Capacity Management 58, 69, 88
CEOs 6
Change Management 58, 69
characteristics, departmental 70–4, *96*
charge-back 7

charters 23–6
charts 16, *77*, 78, 81–2, *96*
checklists 37
communication 10, 56–7, 85
Communications Standards Officer 10
comparison spreadsheets 49–50, 60
compatibility 88
complaints 10
conferences 37
confidentiality 85–6
conformance 9–10, 49–50
construction knowledge, departmental 20
consultation 23, 37
Continual Improvement 68
Continual Service Improvement (ITIL v3) 58, 68
Contract Management 40, *56*
contracts 86
Customer Management 67, 69
customers 38
    information on 57
    interfaces 85
Customer Support 68, 69

Data and Information Management 56
decision-making 9
Demand Management 58
departmental characteristics 70–4, *96*
departmental construction knowledge 20
departmental parameters 23–6, 48–50, 55, 59–61, 65, *95*, *96*
departmental structure 4–12, 65–74
departmental templates *68*, *70*, 78, *96*, 99, 103–4
Departmental Units 65, 66–70, *96*
discussions 54, 55
documentation 5, 9, 50, 61, 65, 95

collating 20
FTs 31–2, 38–41

education *41*, 69
Egypt, ancient, social structure 4–5, 6–7, 8, 71–2
employees *see* staff
Event Management 58
expansion 88
experts 37

farmers 5, 8, *72*
feedback 50, 61
finance 10, 56
food-gathering 8
founders 6
FTs *see* Fundamental Tasks
function, definition 29
functionality 89
Fundamental Tasks 15–16, 23–5, 80, 81, 86–7, 88, *95*, *96*, 104
    characteristics 71–2, 74
    in Departmental Units 65, 66
    identifying 29–32, 35–41
    into phases 94
    rationalizing 45–50
    relationships 54–5

gap analysis 94
gaps in service 38
Gateways 95
goals 25, *26*, 48, 65
Governance Management *39*, *56*
government officials 4, 5, 6, *72*

human resources (HR) 37, *41*, 59, 68, 69

impacts 85
implementation 93–6
improvement 58–9, 68
Incident Management 31, *32*, 58

incompatibility 88
industry associations 37
Information Security Management *56*
institutes 37
instructions, work 86–7, 88, *96*
Integrity Management 67, 69
interfaces 85
IT departments 38
ITIL compatibility 88
ITIL Financial Management component (*Service Strategy*) 10
ITIL Fundamental Tasks 15–16, 23–5, 80, 81, 86–7, 88, *95*, *96*, 104
    characteristics 71–2, 74
    in Departmental Units 65, 66
    identifying 29–32, 35–41
    into phases 94
    rationalizing 45–50
    relationships 54–5
    see also non-ITIL Fundamental Tasks
ITIL guidelines 10, 22, 24, 29
    see also ITIL v2 publications; ITIL v3 publications
ITIL processes 24, 48
ITIL projects 20
ITIL sub-tasks 35, 37
ITIL v2 publications 37, 69, 95, 99
ITIL v3 publications 29, *36*, 37, 58, 68, 69, 94, 95
    Fundamental Tasks 30
    Service Operation and *Service Strategy* 10
    templates 103–4
IT Service Continuity Management 59

job descriptions 85–6, *96*
job titles 81

knowledge, departmental construction 20
Knowledge Management 9, 58

legalities 56
local interest groups 37

maintenance 89
management 6
managers, senior 6
map, phased approach 93–5
marketing and sales 7
merchants 5, 7, *72*
metrics 86, *87*
mission statements 15, 23, 24, 25–6, 65
mobility, social 5
MTAS 86, *87*
MTBS 86, *87*
MTTP 86, *87*

needs analysis 89
networking 37
non-ITIL Fundamental Tasks 35–41, 45–50, *95*
    see also ITIL Fundamental Tasks

office workers 8
operational activities 10, 57
Operations Management 67
organizational charts 16, *77*, 78, 81–2, *96*
organizational plans 78–80, 81–2, 94, *96*
organizations
    benefits of small 54
    as figurehead 6
ownership, total cost of 10

PAD methodology 37, 38
parameters 23–6, 48–50, 55, 59–61, 65, *95*, *96*
performance metrics 86, *87*
personality 54, 56, 57, 58, 59, 66
Pharaoh 4, 5, 6, *72*
phased approach map 93–5
phases 93–6
planning 38
plans 78–80, 81–2, 94, 95, *96*
pressure 86
PRINCE2 20

problems 38, 58
Process and HR Management 68
Process Design and Management *40*, 59, 69
processes 24, 28, 29, 86–7, 88, *96*
production staff 8
project advisers 20
Project Advisory Board 20
project management 9, 19–20
project teams 19–20
pyramid structure 4–12

qualifications for staff 7, 56

records, keeping 5
    see also documentation
Release and Deployment Management 58
repetitive step groups 19
reports 50, 61, 89
Request Fulfilment 58
resources 16, 85–9, *96*
responses 50, 61
return on investment (ROI) 10, *56*
risk analysis 9

sales and marketing 7
scalability 88
scribes 5, 7, *72*
secrecy/security 85–6
sellers 5, 7, 85, 89
seminars 37
senior managers 6
servants 5, 8, *72*
Service Asset and Configuration Management 56
Service Catalogue Management 57
Service Delivery (ITIL v2) 99
Service Desk 10–11, 57, *58*
service improvement 58–9, 68
Service Integrity 69, *70*, *79*
Service Level Management 56, 57

Service Management department structure *11*, 12
Service Operation (ITIL v3) 10
Service Operations 10, 69, *80*
Service Planning 68, 69, *70*, *79*
Service Portfolio Management *57*
Service Strategy (ITIL v3) 10
Service Support 69, *80*
Service Support (ITIL v2) 99
7-Step Improvement Process 69
size of organization 54
skills, staff 7, 54, 56
slaves 5, 8
SM Governance Management *39*, *56*
social mobility 5
software 88–9
soldiers 4, 6, *72*
spreadsheets, comparison 49–50, 60
staff 5, 8, 25, 38, 54, 57
    production 8
    qualified 7, 56
step groups, repetitive 19
storekeepers 5
stress 86
structure, departmental 4–12, 65–74
sub-tasks 35, 37
suite solutions 88

Supplier Management *56*
suppliers 5, 7, 85, 89
support staff 5, 8
support tasks 10–12

Task Packs, Associated Fundamental *see* AFTPs
Tasks, Fundamental *see* Fundamental Tasks
TCO 10
teams 19–20, 54
technologies 10, 54, 57, 87–9, *96*
templates *68*, *70*, 78, *96*, 99, 103–4
terms of reference 23–6
traders 5, 7
training 56, 57

upgrades 89
usability 88–9

vendors 5, 7, 85, 89

weaknesses 38
work instructions 86–7, 88, *96*
workers
    office 8
    skilled 5, 7
    see also staff